Spo
Poe

June 2004
Mary Ashton
pages 79-89

In Silent Thoughts

Edited by Steve Twelvetree

Spotlight Poets

First published in Great Britain in 2004 by
SPOTLIGHT POETS
Remus House
Coltsfoot Drive
Peterborough
PE2 9JX
Telephone: 01733 898102
Fax: 01733 313524
Website: www.forwardpress.co.uk

SB ISBN 1 84077 112 7

Foreword

As a nation of poetry writers and lovers, many of us are still surprisingly reluctant to go out and actually buy the books we cherish so much. Often when searching out the work of newer and less known authors it becomes a near impossible mission to track down the sort of books you require. In an effort to break away from the endless clutter of seemingly unrelated poems from authors we know nothing or little about; Spotlight Poets has opened up a doorway to something quite special.

In Silent Thoughts is a collection of poems to be cherished forever; featuring the work of twelve captivating poets each with a selection of their very best work. Placing that alongside their own personal profile gives a complete feel for the way each author works, allowing for a clearer idea of the true feelings and reasoning behind the poems.

The poems and poets have been chosen and presented in a complementary anthology that offers a variety of ideals and ideas, capable of moving the heart, mind and soul of the reader.

Steve Twelvetree

Contents

The Authors
& Poems

Albert Russo

A bilingual author, Albert Russo writes in both English and French, his two 'mother tongues'. He is the recipient of many awards, such as The American Society of Writers Fiction Award, The British Diversity Short Story Award, several New York Poetry Forum Awards, Amelia Prose and Poetry awards and the Prix Colette, among others. He has also been nominated for the W B Yeats and Robert Penn Warren poetry awards. His work, which has been praised by James Baldwin, Pierre Emmanuel, Paul Willems and Edmund White, has appeared worldwide in a dozen languages. His African novels have been favourably compared to V S Naipaul's work, which was honoured with the Nobel Prize for Literature in 2001. He is a member of the jury for the Prix Européen and sat in 1996 on the panel of the prestigious Neustadt Prize for Literature, which often leads to the Nobel Prize. His most recent novels: in English: *Zany, Zapinette New York, Mixed Blood* and *Eclipse Over Lake Tanganyika* all with Domhan Books (NY); in French: *L'Amant De Mon Père* (Ed Le Nouvel Athanor), *Zapinette À New York, Zapinette Chez Les Belges, L'Ancêtre Noire,* all three with Editions Hors Commerce (Paris).

Excerpted from Martin Tucker's Preface to Albert Russo's novels 'Mixed Blood' and 'Eclipse Over Lake Tanganyika' (both published by Domhan Books in New York):

'*Albert Russo's* work has many distinctive qualities. 'Mixed Blood' and 'Eclipse Over Lake Tanganyika' are especially distinguished by Russo's startlingly precise grasp of the historic period of mid-twentieth-century Central Africa. In this sense, his work bears twinship to V S Naipaul's (Nobel prize winner) 'A Bend In The River'. Such a time no longer exists because one history has changed and another has happened, and still another is happening under our ticking hours. Like his predecessor Naipaul, Russo has captured the attitudes of his white colonialists, his black politicians of various hues of moderation and extremity, and painted a seemingless timeless portrait of a naive American Peace Corps volunteer. (Perhaps naiveté is the one constant in the history of change.) Again, like Naipaul, Russo is compassionate and satiric but unlike his British counterpart, Russo holds out hope that messages of goodness and idealism and decency remain within hearing, that they remain to be recorded in a different and deeper key in another time. Rooted in a past time, 'Mixed Blood' and 'Eclipse Over Lake Tanganyika' have an undeniable relevance to contemporary time.'

The author's literacy website: www.albertrusso.com

The Beauty Of Symmetry

Maybe there is a biological explanation
maybe it is just an aesthetic rule
that God or whosoever has created
the animal kingdom decided that
we should all be that way
I cannot believe it is the result
of a sheer accident.
Why do we have two eyes
separated by a nose
two arms and two legs
in perfect symmetry
when our innards are set
at random, or so it appears?
It's as if that deity or nature
or however you may wish to call it
wanted to hide
the functions of life
the way we do when
we build a car
concealing its motor
under a hood
and making sure
the outer body
is as pleasing to the eye
as we can render it.
Look at the ugliest of reptilians
and you will find that common trait.
What would we have looked like
if we just had a transparent
envelope covering our entrails?
Would we still be beautiful?

Heart Seizure

The plane was late
a snowstorm
drowned the atmosphere
into curtains of tight flakes
and the tarmac
was laced with frost
that's when I find winter's games
most imaginative
it's like the thoughts
of 6 billion human beings
are mingling at last
in an apocalyptic feast
no one is spared
no one is privileged
and everybody
gets the same treatment
it looks as if they are
on a collision course
but no one is hurt either
for they all end
in the same fashion
kissing the ground
I was expecting a dear friend
but all of a sudden
my mind went blank
white like the whirlwind
that kept blowing
over our heads
I felt that ice
had replaced
the blood in my arteries
and that nothing mattered any longer
my friend's features
blurred in my mind
as I breathed my last breath.

Metal

Quick, pass me that knife
it cries out: I need to tear open
a piece of your flesh
and it's pointing at my left thigh.
The battle is lost even before it starts,
for the muscles beckon to it
with prurient expectation.
So what was the use
of working out so much,
sculpting my body as if it
were competing for the world title?
Schwarzie, it's all your fault,
I wanted to become the man you are
and have a taste
of the American dream
you no longer need to exercise
or appear in your bathing trunks;
the women love you,
inside out, so to speak
and they now count in the millions,
fantasising about that hunk
who's now Governor of California.
Yes, you've come a long way
but you will soon be held accountable
before the people of your state.
The knife draws circles around my skin
and I get goose pimples
at the thought that it will
plunge its metallic tongue
into my body.
It's playing a sadistic game
and I don't know when
it's going to strike
I cringe and huff
sweat trickles down my armpits
and I begin to shiver
in spite of the high temperature.
Funny, there's a gush now
and fresh blood oozes out of me
but I don't feel a thing.

Wishful Thoughts

On that broken twig
a bird has alighted
and starts cooing
as if to me alone
I'm a child again
wishing it would never stop.
Closing my eyes
I listen to the lullaby
and see a sky filled
with stardust
then the river of life
from which
silver fish bounce
out of the fountain-waves
it is now raining
flowers over my head
wiping out every
remnant thought
of war and misery.
How I would like
to congeal this instant
of happiness
and never awake
to the horrors of this world
I pray the gods
for a miracle to happen
to let the birds take over
our planet and impose on us
some of the tenets
our great men have
written but which
we seem to forget
the moment we get up
in the morning.
Or maybe the dolphins
should rule us
showing the way
to peace and forgiveness
and mankind would
then listen more closely
to the music of the soul.

Deliverance

She fell into
a drop of blood
and her world suddenly
brightened up
the colour was so vivid
playing with the light
in a rainbow of reds
now the shade of coral
now of vermilion
with, in-between,
flashes of indigo
it felt so warm
that she believed
nothing could hurt her
anymore
and she was right
for the bullet
had reached her
smack between
her lovely blue eyes

Lady Of Nature

She wore a live scarab
as a pendant
and a pair of earrings
studded with fireflies.
At first I thought
what a cruel thing to do
then I noticed her fingers
two rings on both hands
each one adorned
with a ladybird
of a different hue
they too seemed poised
on the brink of flying away
a bracelet of plaited elephant hairs
was coiled around her upper arm.
At dusk she strolled in her garden
and I heard her whisper
to the roses and the dahlias,
bidding them good night
as if each one of them
was a person
then, when the moon appeared,
she said: 'Now, my loved ones,
you may all retire,
tomorrow will be another
joyful day for all of us.'
And out flew the scarab, the fireflies
and the ladybirds,
rejoining their abode
among the flowers.

Sleuth

She had the eerie impression
she was being spied upon
that the foliage was alive
with a hundred pairs of eyes
it was so dark in the brush
as she stood on the edge of the cliff
watching the breakers below
and the frothing grey horizon
she felt sandwiched between
a wall of periscopes
and the platinum immensity
she held her breath lest
she should be engulfed
by either one of them
then panic gripped her
it was those eyes again
invisible yet so present
the sky hung low
black with clouds
and they too kept watching her
as if to wait for her imminent fall
then a howl rent the air
when she came to
the brush was covered with snow
a million eyelets were shimmering
gazing at her benevolently.

Haiku Solitude

She's like an oyster
stranded on top of a rock
no flesh, no pearl, no life

she's like a shadow
hovering over sand dunes
and blinding the sun

a cry in the desert
under freezing temperatures
between Earth and moon

As a little girl
she used to play with ants
diverting their tracks

her parents acted
as if she didn't exist
an unwanted child

the meaning of love
was as foreign to her as
the isle of Fiji

one day she decided
to visit that island
and turned colour-blind.

Of Love And Freedom

I'm entrenched in you
as an infant in his mother
outside, all is war

how dependent I feel
craving for you to come by
killer solitude

I know someone
who lives alone and feels free
free not to love or be loved

a day without music
is a day without water
and I without you

the smile of a child
is a gift from Heaven
just look around

joy, as illusive
as a butterfly kiss
catch it when you can

how free are we?
It's a matter of degree
so much less than a bird

Marj Busby

I took up writing after attending three courses at the Adelaide University Night School, when aged 50. One of my daughters asked me to accompany her, and this I did with interest. Much to my surprise and pleasure the lecturer often picked my pieces out for discussion each week.

After this I started writing for the Australian magazines; letters, to begin with then true articles. The only one that wanted poetry was 'Aussie Post' and they had to be of an Australian nature. I was lucky to have the two I sent, picked out for publication, and instead of money, as usual, I was sent two poetry books by the Australian Bush Laureate 'Book of the Year' award winner, Jim Haynes, who was then writing for 'Aussie Post'; he also sent me two letters, and allowed me to put a couple of his poems on my own web site.

When I had exhausted the Australian market, I turned to Britain where I was born, having emigrated to Australia in 1964 with my husband and four children. I then wrote a lot for 'The Best of British' a monthly magazine. I had had one article in 'The People's Friend' in Scotland. Later I started writing poetry and have been published in several different anthologies.

I thoroughly enjoy writing poetry, which seems to come naturally to me. I also write fiction short stories. I have never, so far, had any published except two on the BBC Kent web site along with several poems. I have also written on other BBC web sites but not so many as Kent.

I have two short stories with the BBC 'Reading for Radio' department They have not returned these in a hurry, so I am hopeful at least one may be picked out to be read on Radio 4.

I now have twelve grandchildren and although getting older and suffering with osteoarthritis of my legs, I find the Internet and writing poetry a good substitute for not being able to walk far, and with God's grace, I hope I will be able to continue this for many more years.

Searching For Rainbow's End

I always look at rainbows.
Fascinating the colours.
Wondering will I ever find the
rainbow's end?

Looking up at the sky
I long to be able to reach,
feel the touch of the arc.
Will I find Heaven there?

Sometimes I dream I have,
as I lay on the grass.
I find beauty there,
such a feeling of grace.

I don't want a crock of gold.
all I want is peace for
this troubled world.
In vain maybe.

People tell me I am
wasting my time.
Still, I will always
look at rainbows.

The Ritual Of Death

Shadowy figures dancing in the forest
Naked women seen through diaphanous gowns
Long flowing hair swinging to the music
Played by men on long bamboo instruments.
Gradually the dancing became more frenetic
Until the gowns clung to the female sweating bodies
Then some naked men joined the group
Gradually encircling the white-robed nymphs.
Twirling and gyrating coming together woman to man
Suddenly a bell peals, the dancers stop and fall.
On the ground the nymphs become twisting snakes
The naked men turning into animals
Wildly the snakes curled around leopard bodies,
Crunching, squeezing. Another ritual finished.

The Misdeed

Over the hills I roamed free today,
For I earlier, I knew I would have to pay.
Thinking thoughts, best not remembered,
Suffering for the misdeeds, dismembered.

That man whom I killed, showing no remorse,
For all his mistreatment and worse.
He looked so handsome when first we met
Many years later his actions that did upset.

Trying to forget that penetrating knife,
Plunged into his heart, after years of strife.
Now I dream of that awful deed I perpetrated,
Dearly paying by dreams, feeling petrified.

Now I am free to wander the countryside
Having served my sentence, paid by being inside.
Prison walls, cells, inmates and criticism,
Praying for forgiveness, knowing empiricism.

Now I think I am able to face the world,
Having had time to purge, my theoretical sword.
So I am making a new life in compensation,
Hoping that my years left, will bring me absolution.

The Last Of The Wine

Red the wineglass
Gleaming in the candlelight.
White the tablecloth
Silver the cutlery.
We drank a toast
To our past life.
Did I see a tear glisten
Realising it was the end
Of our love affair,
Beginning so torridly,
Ending so peacefully?
Our glasses clinked,
We downed our wine.
There was nothing to say,
We both knew how to end.
An evening of sorrow. No!
Mainly a drinking of red wine
To end our life together.

The Lake

Raindrops, falling as tears
pouring down her face
as she walks towards the lake.
Trying hard to allay her fears.

Nearing the water, her steps falter
looks back at the house behind
no signs of anyone following.
She wades into the cold water.

Gradually it covers her head.
One last panic, shall she succumb
into those murky depths, deciding.
Bubbles, choking, she sinks, like lead!

The Gift Of Tongues

The gift of tongues
What is this treasure?
Why drinking champagne,
It gives so much pleasure.

Poured at every celebration,
Voices do rise in happy unison
As people laugh, talk, jig a dance
Loving every minute of consummation.

The Ending

Faint voices, pain, bright lights I see.
All my children are gathered around me.
They think because I am quiet, I cannot hear
But they grieve and whisper, 'Isn't she a dear?'
I've had a good life, seen a lot of sights.
Pain is easing now, there is a dimming of lights.
I know death is nigh, I have reached ninety-nine.
Oh! How I wish they would not pine.
They kiss my old and withered face,
As I struggle towards that other place.
Striving for speech, to say, 'I love you all,'
As upon my skin their tears do fall.
I think they heard my whispered plea
Now I am floating, I feel so free!

My Servant

My mind transcends all life.
Making my pen my servant.
Bringing forth ideas, hopes, longings,
Writhing, to recall things rife.
Letters appear on a blank page.
Arriving as if by a magic hand.
Making the words appear miraculously.
Releasing ideas from their cage.
I lovingly cherish each word
Appearing before my eyes.
A kaleidoscope written in pictures,
I bow down to my pen, my servant, my lord.

My Grandfather

The sea was extremely rough
The day the sailor went below
To lay a line across the channel,
In those days things were tough.
He wore a diver's suit, as he was bade,
Along with one or two others
They laid their line, against the odds
So that communication could be made.
Alas one day when the seas were bad
He did not return when the line was pulled,
His cord had snagged upon a rock.
This made my grandmother very sad.
They finally did his body find
Amongst that, by then, serene sea.
He was laid to rest in a quiet grave
The memory oft stays in my mind.

My Dreams

Memories of my many dreams
Transport me into satisfaction, actually hurled
I think back to my former schemes
And am transposed into a lovely world.
Glowing the sky, red the sunset at night
Also glowing the hot midday sun
The stars that shone so bright,
And the moonlight faintly just begun.
Mountains towering over my head,
Such white snow making many a fatality.
I glory in these memories not dead
Even if some are dreams of reality.
Now I must remember all of them, I'll explain
For never can I experience them truly, again.

Memories

That beautiful blue sky
Feathered, cotton wool-clouded,
Reminds me of snowy mountains
And travels where they abounded.
That eerie dark sky
Where some stars shone,
Reminds me of happy nights
Times that have now gone.
That darkening black sea
Lightened by the golden moon,
Reminds me of my grandad
A sailor who died too soon.
That lovely turquoise sea
With gentle dips and swells,
Reminds me of happy holidays
And different seaside smells.
That verdant green place
Where our family had fun,
Reminds me of childhood
Before adulthood had begun.
These golden memories of the past
When all seemed perfect then,
Reminds me that things can't last
It's hard to know just when.

Love?

Thinking back I do make haste
To taste your mouth again and again.
Feeling the ripeness of your taste,
As your lips descending, remain.
I hold you so close once more,
Feeling that I will never let you go.
Clinging mouth to mouth, feeling to my core
I cannot lose you, I'll never let you know.
How much I treasure you in my life,
Loving you as I have never ever felt,
To lose you would wound me like a knife.
Avoid this I will, doing anything not to melt.
So together we will always be, I trust.
As with dagger deep in your heart, I thrust.

Lovely Sights

Rainbows and butterflies
Both of these fascinate me,
Flowers, scent and tree
People rave about all three.

But to me the butterfly is the one
That makes my body want to fly,
And coloured rainbows that make me try
To reach in vain, disappearing, I cry

So rainbows and butterflies
Will forever make my heart leap.
So sun and rain shine and wet do keep
My heart happy, not letting my eyes seep.

Looking For Him

Faces alight with wonder.
Changing to craven fear,
As the golden orbs of heat
Made eyes burn with tear.

They had prayed for a sign
That their God was not a dream,
Thinking that to question this
Would make blind eyes; they scream!

Heaven's Elements

As the rain came in a shower
A rainbow appeared in the sky
Such colours; one wonders why,
Are elements showing their power
Like small plants beginning to flower?
One child reaches up to touch, to try,
When hands can't reach, she gives a cry.
Parents soothe, say, 'It is only a bower.'

The rain now starts with all its might,
Gone the upturned faces, seeing not a flying raven
Flying, as people scatter to reach a safe space,
Being no longer able to see colours so bright.
A church nearby provides a safe haven.
They stay to pray. In this heavenly place.

Going Back

As I entered through the old oaken doors
Of the old broken-down mansion
My body received a shock. I felt as if I was
Coming back to somewhere I knew.
There was a dampness in the air, a feeling of decay.
It was an effort to press myself forward.
Making myself climb the rickety stairs I turned right,
What made me do this was an inner feeling
Of compulsion, facing me a door, I just had to enter
Why? I silently asked, as the room was large
With faded, hanging curtains. Only an old table was in view.
Upon it lay just one old book, beautifully bound.
Reading the words inside, I suddenly realised
I was reading my own passages. Somehow I was back
In a former time. In that life I was an author of renown.
Realising this I thought, reincarnation. I was indeed the
Person who had written this great book.
Who was I? I cannot tell, who would believe it?
Leaving the old house with a feeling of elation
Such as I had not felt for so many years.
I knew what I must do. Write again. Masterpieces,
As I did in my former life.

Floating Thoughts

Thoughts floating away, like feathers in a breeze
Where do they go? These treasures of mind.
Do any ears hear them? Even a whisper.
Does anyone reply?

I heard one once, coming down from the leaves
Blown from an autumn tree.
Whispering a message, which listening,
    My ear faintly caught.

The voice that lit a smile on my face, was
A message from an angel, murmuring
Loving sounds, that made my heart sing.
    For it was also a kiss.

Fields Of Clover

Down in the fields of clover
I spent happy hours with my lover,
As we lay in the mauve-coloured bed
We dreamed of the day we would be wed.

Then the war took him to places bad,
Alone, down in the fields of clover, sad.
My body aching for his gentle touch,
Which was there, only in my mind as such.

A bullet pierced his heart in battle, you see
So he never returned, his arms to enfold me.
So lonely, I shared the memory of my lover
Down in the fields of clover.

Maria Ann Cahill

My poetry addresses the way we deal with our world.

I belong to the Grimsby Writers Network Group; we meet every month to discuss new writings and challenges, sharing openly any problems, if anyone has had any difficulties, we discuss how best to tackle these. Improvements any fellow writer may have to add are talked over too. Basically, this is a valuable, trusting, wonderful group of not only writers, but great friends also. Our meeting is held at The Point in Doncaster, a truly wonderful art centre.

The most interesting of our workshops was the author of crime fiction, David Fine. This for us all, appeared to have shown a great deal of insight into the creative mind, expanding in the fiction field of writing.

I was born in the West Middlesex hospital in London on 27th March 1954 but was separated from my natural mother at the age of three. Although I was born in England, because my mother was an Irish girl, she took me back to Ireland where she became a nursery nurse so she could take care of me and pay for our keep. She was later advised to give me up for adoption and was told I would be better off and better looked after. They said they had a couple who would be interested in me. To cut a long story short, I never did get over being separated from my mother and was later taken to hospital suffering from a nervous disorder. My adoptive mother was cruel and cold towards me.

It took me twenty-two years to find my mother, the adoption agency would not relent and when they finally did, my mother had passed away. My new-found family members have all told me that I was a much wanted and loved baby. I had always felt this and believe it to have been my driving force. I dedicate this work to my mum.

I love writing and I hope that you enjoy my work. I know my mum would want you to as she has been my strength. I have two wonderful grown up children and now a little grandson who is simply adorable.

My work has appeared in various women's magazines over the years. There are also a number of anthologies published by Poetry Now, Women's Words, Triumph House, Anchor Books and Strong Words holding my work. Some of my short stories appear in books published by New Fiction. There are also four Spotlight books holding collections of my work.

I Watched

(A Rondeau poem)

I watch the birds high up in the tree,
Some tilt their heads in watch of me.
Different kinds of whistling sounds I hear,
I try to gain their confidence, only two or three come near.
The beautiful shine upon each bird's feathers I see,
I will go inside and let them be.

I watch from my window now to see,
Pretty little birds, one, two and three,
Oh! My heart is filled with glee,
To watch them pick at the bird table of seed,
Even though they lose some to my grass weed!

They bathe in the sand bath so happy and free,
I will go and let them be,
Now I can take my rest contentedly.

Her Love Of Moonlit Water

(Pantoum Poem)

The shimmering light of the moon shone across the water.
She watched in thought from her window.
With her fear of strangers in the dark,
She wished she had felt safe enough to go out.
She watched in thought from her window,
The gentle rain started to patter upon the glistening water,
She wished she had felt safe enough to go out,
She was remembering strangers could not be trusted.
The gentle rain started to patter upon the glistening water,
With her fear of strangers in the dark,
She was remembering strangers could not be trusted,
The shimmering light of the moon shone across the water.

Infinity With Life

An infinity of stars and the song of the beach
I slept beneath
What wondrous beauty
A midnight blue, of seeming like velvet
This blanket covered me

The thrash of the ocean
With the twinkling of winking stars
Combined

I talk of the summer nights
The softness, of the cotton feel, of sweet grass
Used as my pillow

The old oak tree that spreads her branches in span
As though sharing her mother-like love of the land
It would seem that without the blessing of nature
We would surely fold up
For without any sparkle how could we survive?

This morning it is five-thirty and I see the flight of birds
They head towards a housing estate
They look to see, if there, food be
Then they fly back for the cover of the tree

It is no wonder the artist paints great beauty
The unicorn and the beautiful maiden
They, fly over the sky
The waters of all the Earth meet
Animals run to greet and bleat

Humans live in amongst the grass and trees
No fear is ever near
Just peace and love, with serenity
Ah, such a world we all seek
Even though it is here already, at our feet.

Innocent Angel

Innocent angel falling down, down and down,
Travelling the journey to Earth,
You are born.

Born to a world so fast,
As you come from your nest,
Soon to bear a family crest,
Waves of a different kind now surround you.
You are born.

Innocent angel who fell down, down and down,
Through waves of pushes,
Though you know your mother's voice,
Your mother's loving touch,
You know you have entered Earth,
You are born.

Nature made it so,
That you would bless your parents with joy,
You know more than they.
Innocent angel you chose your way,
For now, there is the shock,
Of the push and cry of landing,
You are born.

Planet Star,
Spark of God,
Breath of man,
Speak your joy,
You are born.

From the day you are born,
Nourish your child, they say,
Do they listen to you?
To your communication, to your knowledge?
You are born.

Do we ever listen to the baby?
What about the one true gift,
The one the baby was born with?
Even in our Lord's time we humans doubted this.
You are born.

Your ability to see, to know at birth
Already of the planet Earth,
To open the door time and time again,
To show us this unconditional almighty powerful love,
You are born.

Safely Tucked Up

(Italian sonnet)

It snowed outside while she was safely tucked up in bed,
Thoughts came to her of those cold and lonely.
She began to pray, 'Please look after them, oh Lord, wholly
Keep them safe oh Lord and shine Mr Moon brightly.'
She said her prayers in such earnest,
Her heart was so pure and true, to pray hard, to her seemed best,
Maybe her prayers will be answered some day.
Oh! Lord, please let your angels come to care.

She cuddled into her pillow and relaxed to sleep,
To her, the lonely cold night for those outside, just was not fair.
She got up and went to her bedroom window, to at the snowfall peep.
She was only seven with her teddy under her arm and a ribbon
in her hair.

The Beggar

(Rondelet)

A face hidden,
Tucked inside a coat to keep warm,
A face hidden,
To talk to him, my mother had forbidden,
I said a prayer, to chase harm,
I threw to him, my lucky charm,
A face hidden.

The Kiss Of The Angel

(A triolet poem)

The kiss of the angel brushed my cheek,
Light winds moved across the sky.
Clouds made the day, for some bleak,
The kiss of the angel brushed my cheek,
It made me feel humble and meek.
Clouds shape the formation of steps as I draw nigh,
The kiss of the angel brushed my cheek,
Light winds moved across the sky.

The Matter Of The Moment

No matter what,
No matter where,
No matter the matter,
I will always be there,
With my pen and my paper,
The matter of the moment,
Will be there forever.

Justice will be served,
Understanding will come through,
For the matter of that moment,
Will shine just for you.

Like a film taken by your camcorder,
My mind will run it through,
And the matter of the moment,
Will develop upon paper.

Just tell me your reason,
Just tell me your preference,
And I will write with seasoning,
With a taste of a different kind.

While your mind unwinds,
With the pleasure of the treasure,
Of the matter of the moment,
Kept forever!

Frank Bruno

Twenty-five years in the highlight,
Twenty-five years in my heart,
A boxer of talent,
Now it's a length of relent,
I love it when you laugh,
I love it,
When I see you now,
As you say, 'Come on Kojack.'
When you were playing golf.

Ten years of marriage,
As it breaks today,
Does not take your cornerstones away.

You're Frank Bruno,
You lived alone in your mansion,
And slept in your own boxing ring,
Well Frank, you are still our main man.

Respect you have in this our world,
We need you to know,
You're our tomorrow,
You're our future,
You gave us a ring of gold,
You were not sold out.

By your side your public wait,
It doesn't have to be a boxing date,
Your face,
Your grace,
Frank Bruno, your space,
'You know what I mean, Harry?'

Only Four Foot!

(A sonnet)

The rooms of her house were small,
As she sat in thought of decoration,
She didn't really want to decorate at all!
Still, all the same, she would have to make preparation.
This was a small woman; she was only four foot in height.
She would need some stepladders without a doubt,
Poor thing had a great fear of height, but it had to be done.
She had no family to help her out,
Many, many, quotes she had seen, all too expensive.
She got the dust sheets out to make ready,
Now in thought, she sat intensive,
She propped the stepladder against the wall to keep it steady,
Then gingerly she climbed, with paint pot in hand,
So high up, she seemed to stand!

Searching For You

(Written when I was in Scotland looking over the beach, just thinking of my mum . . . I had found my two brothers and one sister. I was visiting them for the first time!)

Twenty-two years of searching for you,
with a strong urge and sheer determination,
I kept pushing closed doors.
Questions and answers fill my mind,
finding to God, you have gone.

Looking over the deep ocean tide,
feeling a world, vast and wide.
Catching sight of a rainbow,
overhead the seagull flies.

I wipe a spillage of tears from my eyes,
and you are there!
Are you the wind that blows my hair?
Are you the rainbow overhead?
Are you the drop of dew?
Is this essence I now feel,
really you?

A peace grew within my heart,
a gentle breeze brushed my cheek,
I could feel you!
I knew you were there.
My heart grew warm,
I knew your love, the specialness
of you.

Searching for you,
my sweet mother,
and finding you forever.
I wanted so much,
to give you a physical cuddle.

When my brothers,
and sister I hold,
I know I will hold you.
Your love runs through,
yes, you are,
the wind that blows my hair,
and the rainbow overhead!

Comets

We took a late night walk,
During which we had a lovely talk,
The dogs were with us,
Waiting for the next thrown stick,
Excited by the play.
'Look!' you shouted, 'look up quick.'
We both looked up into the sky.

Two large flashes of fire-like light,
Lit up the night,
They flew across the sky,
Each followed by a wonderful glowing trail.

It was a spectacular sight,
Those two comets of the night,
Excitement filled both our souls,
In awe of such beautiful wonder.

That night, my daughter and I
Our minds had opened to such cosmic beauty,
The next day,
There it was on the news,
Two comets were marked in time,
Noted in a book.

Oh how glad I was,
That you had asked me to go out,
And how glad I was of your shout.

Bless Him Oh Lord

(Dedicated to my little grandson Ben)

Bless him, oh Lord,
To know his mother's unconditional love,
And when it is time to close Earth's gate,
He need never wonder.

My soul cries its bitter-sweet tears,
Now knowing, only, if only,
A love unrequited upon Earth,
For someone separated a wanting child,
At its tender age of three,
From the splash of rainbows,
Of magic, of mother's love.

Bless oh Lord, to teach 'Golden Hair',
Bless, oh bless, to teach him deeply,
Of his mother's undying love.

I see only white clouds and blue sky,
The soft grass bearing an infant,
Playing with others of the same,
And nuns who called, 'Maria'
I now know to be my name.

All I have that is real has gone above.
Now white clouds I watch and dream,
'Golden Hair',
Know of your mother's unconditional love,
Your mother's joy,
In you,
Our baby boy.

Legacy

(Dedicated to my dad)

My father left me a legacy,
See.
A room full of books to read,
Seed.
Intelligence was always his way,
Say.
My father spoke, read, and wrote different languages,
Manages.
He believed so much in the mind,
Kind.

Diana Mudd

 Devon-born, Diana Mudd is a versatile poet of many variations and styles. Ranging from the deep and serious to frivolous humour, she puts spiritual and romantic inspirations into verse and loves writing poetry for children.

Her poetry is read and enjoyed around the world; she has had many of her poems published in magazines and anthologies and sometimes locally she does poetic readings.

She has written poetry she says, 'for about a thousand years' and the inspirational pleasure of writing verse has never faded. Not only was she inspired to write poetry at a very young age but saw writing as a challenge to master her dyslexia 'though she unashamedly admits to still being a victim of this condition.

She hopes her poetry will encourage, inspire and influence those who struggle with dyslexia to venture forward and never give up trying to do whatever they enjoy doing with the spirit of challenge and achievement rather than accept a despondent, disillusioned and hopeless attitude.

Although she has always written poetry, it is only now in her retirement that she feels able to give her time to doing something with it rather than just play with it as a hobby and interest.

She lives with her husband, David, in Tavistock on the edge of the beautiful National Park.

Among her vast interests, her hobbies include walking, swimming music, opera and ballet.

She says, 'I have always had a great love of nature and life and I enjoy people; I find them to be so very interesting, comical and inspiring. I think one should try to avoid taking life too seriously. Understanding and a healthy sense of humour are essential ingredients to adopting the right attitude of staying young at heart and being positive, progressive and happy.'

How Black Was My Valley?

Deep in the burrowed
gouged-out blackness
in the shadows of time
they sphere-less dwell
in labyrinths long echoes
of pickaxe and shovel and
blinkered pit ponies and old black gold.

Above the dark earth
the black wheels are turning
towering tall o'er the valley steep; and
the mesh wire cage
lifts to a dismal view
from entrance to exit and the bowels of the earth.

Down through the hillsides
raw mists are crawling
consuming the lichen and
the dull yellow gorse,
somewhere on high
the dark winds are gathering
creeping their way through the black grit dust.

Heavily laden they blow,
devouring the hillsides
through the mountains of slag
as black as the night, and the silt-crawling rivers
wash thick down the valley
eating black slurry and swallowing grime.

No mercy accorded
nor honour bestowed
to the colourless landscapes
or the painted black hills,
nor the groups on the pit head
scarcely daring a breath
as they wait to see who is dead or alive
from flood, or explosion, in the black tunnels below.

Daytime or night-time
meet a measureless darkness
as fate grips the valley
in disaster's tight hands,
hour-less days freeze into timeless emotions
echoing only the sound of the turning black wheels.

As the valley mourns gravely
the black-faced dead,
for each corpse that passes
every clasped hand is praying and
all the valley weeps deeply
for those it has taken,
every sound is lament echoing through the black hills.

Love mixed with hate grip
the souls of the grieving;
of the lives ripped apart, and
their broken dreams,
dark shadows fall long
through the cold painted hillsides, and
only an emptiness knocks leaving gravestones behind.

How green was my valley
before the giants invaded and
the rhythm of wheels perpetually turned.
How rich was my valley
beneath wild waving grasses and
green clinging lichen and the bright yellow gorse.

There was gold in the valley
when the giants confronted, and
Welsh voices were ringing
through the green, green hills
then, a blackness descended and
a grimness impeded, and
the green rolling valley sang to a dark dismal tune.

A fear gripped the valley
as black giants were devouring
but joy echoed far
for the feel of black gold, and
laughter was heard
from the little brick houses
sprouting row after row to the tunes of black coal.

So bleak was my valley
in slag heap and slurry,
where sleet winds blew raw
through the rolling black hills, and
the white snow laid grey
in the valley's black memories and
there, in the hillsides,
lay the past and the dead.

Down the valley of song,
sing all the ghosts of the ages, and
infants who waited
by candle's flickering flame
in the smell of the darkness and
the dripping black coal seams and
the numbness that crippled with the dust and the damp.

My valley lay bare and
black to the heavens
oppressive and murky
where black grasses blew and
the hills touched the sky
without end or beginning and
depression claimed its victims
in the darkness of earth.

Now bodiless,
still the Welsh choirs are singing
faint songs of the valleys
that ring down through the hills
where moss cushions fresh
and soft to the treading, and
wild grasses sway green o'er the graves of the dead.

The voices that linger
still ring through the valley
from chapels on high in celestial realms,
from their hearts and their souls
love ever is drifting in echo's ageless reflection,

How black
Was my valley

of long ago.

Another World

Between the barren of the Earth
And distant lands where all worlds meet
Mortals pass into immortality, each heart no more again to beat.

Earth has dismissed their body and soul
Left nothing remaining, save any deed shown,
Or any seed in a lifetime sewn.

Now only Heaven or Hell awaits
If naught lies between,
Ascend or descend, to reside, none there again are seen.

Day or night, no ties, no plan,
All meet in some new world
From which all worlds began.

No lesser, no greater, can each soul lay their claim;
No more or less than deeds recorded on some angel's list,
But be positioned, they, in some other world where no one is missed.

None superior would condemn but would redeem,
If superior they reign,
And, in their forward journey,
All things gain.

Sinking Ships

No anchor needed now
As they quietly slip
Down, down, and drift
Beneath the waves
To their ocean bed
And their last trip.

In the hands of fate
They to the deep commit,
Descending
Into the graveyard of the sea,
Shallow or deep
Unlit.

The sea,
In eerie silent waters,
Secrets of the depths
And dark they keep,
In their descent
They sink
Into an unknown watered realm
Where souls forever sleep.

None can claim them now;
No demand upon their time,
No duty call,
No appointment to keep.

Revenge

Oh,
vengeance sweet,
come, play with me,
churn me
with your sweet delights,
tantalise
my taste buds,
flavour my desire;
I lust
the lust
of temptation's fulfilment.
My mind,
my lips,
my veins
taste the taste of revenge,
taste
the taste of your delicious sweetness.
Come,
I beckon you,
play with my taste buds, amuse me with your will,
sweeten the sap of my desire;
the sap that rises and floats around my tongue,
the sap that drifts around the centre of my mind.
Engage me,
entertain me,
trifle with my possessiveness,
power my craft,
entice me and seduce me
with the sweetness of temptation's honey,
draw me
into your wilfulness
that I may explore your full potential,
your power.
Pleasure me
to exercise your will,
favour me
to savour all your joyous fancies.
Oh, vengeance sweet,
empower me
to serve your purpose well.

Did They?

Did they see the golden light
Just behind the drifting cloud
Did they see the silver in the stars
When the night became their shroud
Did they hear the bugle call,
Did they hear the trumpet sound
When they ascended into glory from their grave upon the ground?

When they went to meet the war
With boots polished to a gloss,
Did they march with hearts triumphant,
Did they see their shining cross,
Did they hear a choir of angels sing
In the peace from Eden's paradise around
When they ascended into glory from their grave upon the ground?

Did all the gates of Heaven swing open,
Did they climb those silent stairs,
Did they feel the heart of Earth was with them
Upon the loving lips of hymns and prayers?
Did they see the face of God,
Did they rejoice at Heaven found,
When they ascended into glory from their grave upon the ground?

When they ascended to their glory
From their grave upon the ground?

Summer's Bouquet

Summer
displays her radiant golden crown
and reigns supreme;
boasting
upon her priceless throne
while gloating
at her vast amount of wealth
spilling
from her overflowing cup.

She
pleasures
in all her assets;
the treasure chest
of nature's abundant riches,
rejoicing
in all of her summer jewels
as she admires her own bouquet.

Wishes

When
bright stars shiver
high upon the Heaven's bough
Earth,
in the hands of God may quiver,
and he, of Earth, who stands below,
may wish all wishes
yet naught deliver.

Sometimes
he loves,
oh he of Earth,
sometimes
he pledges all of Heaven's stars;
sometimes he wishes on night's sky
for that
which to him daytime bars.

Still
man dreams beyond himself
for that which to him can't be cast
and still he measures not his pledge
but denies true worth
to render last.

From
himself he departs to chase,
in depth, his dream
that rests on all his eager vision
that never to him ever clouds or mars,
seeking to catch his perfection in gloss
and denying to himself upon the quest
what can never be his
yet
will still pain him in loss.

When
bright stars shiver
high upon the Heaven's bough,
Earth
in the hands of God may quiver,
and he, of Earth who stands below,
may wish all wishes
yet naught deliver.

Gael Nash

I was born in Glasgow, the daughter of a doctor and a nurse, the eldest of three girls. We migrated to South London when I was four - 'for the weather' my father said! He was a dominant man who did not believe in giving praise. My mother was gentle, artistic and a linguist. We had a strict but happy childhood until she contracted cancer at the age of forty-one and died seven months later. I was fifteen, my sisters twelve and ten.

Life changed dramatically as my father married my mother's older sister nine months on. She was the archetypal wicked stepmother. Life deteriorated rapidly and I started to write poetry as a cathartic exercise.

I was unhappy until I married at the age of twenty-three - a barrister. We were poor but happy and as a Froebel-trained teacher, I worked until our first son, Matthew, was born. Our pattern of life was established, overtaken by motherhood. I felt fulfilled and we went on to have another three children. Again, life was tainted by tragic deaths - my youngest sister, a doctor, and two of our sons. The ripple effect this had on our marriage and our family life was enormous and we went through some very dark years. I began to write again, hoping to ease the pain.

I had been brought up on a diet of 'iambic pentameter' and initially wrote in this form and then in rhyming couplets, but recently have tried to vary my style by learning through poetry workshops and reading.

I love literature and completed a Combined Studies Certificate recently through Kent University at Canterbury. I also have a London University Diploma in Sociology. Literature and poetry have sustained me through depressing times. There is light at the end of the tunnel and at this stage of my life, my husband, son and daughter sustain me with humour and love. I now feel I can express the lighter side of life. We learn as we go and every experience, whether joyful or sad, adds strength - everything has a purpose and life is a steep learning curve - as the modern expression goes!

July

Expectations of summer now fulfilled
stillness in the air.
No breeze disturbing the tranquillity.
The morning haze lifts with the heat of the sun.
Penetrating beams of light
dancing on the vibrant colours of the garden.
Swallows darting in and out of the rafters
searching for food for their young.
Some, sadly prostrate on the ground,
small wings too fragile for suspension.
The ever-present crow and heron
hovering, awaiting their prey.
Sounds of summer, scents of intense pleasure.
An amalgam of peace.
Yet midsummer over, freshness dulled.
Power of nature, red in tooth and claw
pervading seasons uncontrolled by Man
summer hopes receding
autumn and winter in juxtaposition.
Time moving ever ceaselessly, relentlessly
beyond our control.

The Death Of Courtesy

Modern manners leave me cold
None taught and none absorbed
We push and shove and never learn
To take good grace on board.

When driving on a motorway
And dithering in a lane
We're flashed, we're hooted, flashed again
Till panicked and insane.

An unfamiliar sign we see
Impatience on our tail
We signal, we adjust our pace
We drive down hill and dale.

Our shopping trips are burdensome
No courtesies are shown
No facial contact do we see
Just insolence and scorn.

The staff are joking with their peers
Unnoticed there I stand
'My goods are faulty,' I explain
Expressions given - bland.

'I'm sorry' I would like to hear
'We will investigate'
But, no, invisible I am
No response can I create.

My money is refunded
With not a word involved
I'm handed back the cash in hand
Eye contact unresolved.

Courtesy is not that hard
Or verbal interaction
But innate manners are withheld
And give no satisfaction.

Just 'please' and 'thank you' I would hope
Would lighten up the day
A smile, a gesture that would help
To send us on our way.

Our parents taught us how to live
To touch, to talk, to laugh
To listen to each other
From house and home and hearth.

We each deserve some happiness
We each deserve some love
We need to think of others
And true humility prove.

Selective Hearing

My husband's hearing's not too good
From driving cars without a hood
High tonal deafness he has now
My voice alas is not that low.
He tells me that he cannot hear
And lip-reads as he comes up near
Bur when I talk upon the phone
It magnifies and clears the tone.
And when I whisper rude remarks,
'I can hear you talk,' he barks
Selective hearing? Just a touch
Methinks he does protest too much!

NHS Parking

Hospital appointment at three-thirty
Dropped the patient by the door
Went to park the vehicle
Miles away, for sure.

Cars in desperation
Looking for a space
Getting angry with each other
Fighting for each place.

Drivers backing in the roadway
Mouthing to those queuing
Passing on their tickets
Arguments now brewing.

Three are angling for each slot
Unaware of those just walking
Pedestrians fearing for their lives
Human behaviour somewhat shocking.

This all too fifteen minutes
With parking fee to pay
Perhaps private medicine's better
Their car park's *free,* they say!

Memories

Five years on, April ninth
When hearts and lives stood still.
Impossible that time has gone
Seems like yesterday
Yet a life away
The pain not as sharp but still overwhelming.
He would have been thirty-five.
What might have been
What he would have achieved?
The sea has taken him
His body buried undiscovered in its depth.
His plane, his shroud.
Aspirations cut short
Dreams unfulfilled
Life cruel, cutting short ambitions
Parents and siblings left behind, abandoned
Coping with grief, lives bereft
Victims of circumstances beyond control
Memories tinged with sadness, some with humour
A firstborn son, out of sight but forever in mind.

Life Cut Short

A baby boy weighed in at 6lbs and 9 ounces
Slipping silently into this world
A bleak December day in 1969
Forlorn, frail and fragile
Elegantly slender, dark-haired, skin like silk.
Delicate as the finest porcelain.
Disinterested in the breast
Unhappy with the bottle
Difficult to nurture.
Never smiling, never whimpering, never crying
Demanding nothing.
Conforming to a pattern of sleep
Abnormal even at so young an age.
Milk never staying digested in his young body
Absorbing little, growing little
Warm to the touch, but unresponsive.
Eleven weeks old in February
Slipping silently from this world
Cold and at rest
Our precious son.

Smog

Sunday afternoon.
I was ten years old.
The day was calm and peaceful.
Sunday lunch completed
Preparing for Sunday school.
Explosion, suddenness, blackness.
The sun absorbed by a dark menacing sky.
Dismal, dank devilling.
Fog creeping cruelly callously, confining.
A filthy taste overtaking the mouth.
A heaviness filling the nose
Fog camouflaging trees, flowers, soil
Fog in the garden
Fog everywhere
Pitch-black and engulfing
Gloom encircling body and soul
Fear and foreboding
Day turned to night in the blink of an eye
London smog!
The first experience of the taste and smell of fear.

Infancy

'Mummy, Mummy! Come and see!'
Excitement, exhilaration
My four-year-old sister, clamouring for attention.
She had succeeded in climbing into the large pram
Belonging to our younger sister.
My mother responded to her urgent call.
Suddenly, a heartrending scream
Split the silence of the evening
Suspended in limbo.
The youngest sibling, trying to be helpful
Climbed onto a stool
Heaving scalding water from the stove
Drenched her head, her arms, her hands, her body,
Saturating her woollen clothes
Engulfing her small body in steam.
Scissors at the ready
Ripping, removing
Soothing, cleansing, cooling water.
Torso saved, legs restored
Scarring uncontrolled on arm and hairline
Vivid violet, red-raw, dominant
Remaining visible until her premature death.
Four days of howling, sobbing
Found me crouching, clinging to the coats
In the under stairs cupboard
Shutting out the noise and the pain
Forgotten in the heat of the moment
And rightly so.

The Treachery Of Memory

Face gazing out of the window
To the left, the garden next door
A greyhound wandering down the path
Agitating to be released.
To the right, the grey granite roofs of the neighbouring houses
In the Border town where I spent the second and third years of my life.
The sinking, wintry sun stole stealthily between the buildings
Cold and sombre as my mood.
Why was I locked in that afternoon
In a bathroom, white-tiled and clinical?
Other children are sent to their rooms
Not to a public place used by all the family.
It was for disobedience, insubordination
I had refused to greet a maiden aunt.
She had tried to kiss me.
The closeness of her face, scratching and be-whiskered
Had not pleased me.
I had stamped my feet and shouted, 'No!'
Not until tea and supper had been served
Was I allowed my escape.
Contrition expected, apologies accepted
A sad little girl who should have known better.
This I recall in retrospect.
The treachery of memory
My childhood insecurities
Are present in my adult life.
Infantile vocabulary lost in time
But the passion of those feelings lives ever in my heart.

Fear

So many fears
Some real, some without foundation
Fears of war and escalation
Affecting not only local environs
But globally.
Innocent victims wiped out.
Villains of terror going unpunished.
Corporate fear.
Peace no longer within our jurisdiction.
Dislocated world
Personal fear.
Fear of not achieving potential,
Of not succeeding.
Fear of broken relationships
Of impending loss.
Swept away by circumstances and fate.
Is this a self-fulfilling prophecy?
Powers beyond control.
Or nature-nurture?
Environmental changes for good and bad
The threatening power of fear
Omnipresent.

Stormy Weather

Power cuts and power lines down
Winds at eighty miles per hour
Screeching, whining, whispering in down pipes
Dried autumnal leaves swirling in a clockwise direction.
The pond is as powerful in its movement as a storm at sea
With coots and moorhens struggling to keep upright
Sheltering in the shadows of the rushes already battered in the winds
Nature red in tooth and claw
Man's greed for fast cars, fast food, fast communication
The ever growing need to be upwardly and economically mobile
The planet ever battered by the never-ending search for power
Over the sea, the air, in space and under the ocean
Chemically damaging the ozone, precipitating illness
What have we done and what the justification?
We are not ultimately responsible for our own destiny.
Our man-made constructions damaged in the storm
Human lives cut short, hopes curtailed
Trees damaged beyond belief, mobility impaired
Salvaging what we can of this destruction
And hoping for stillness, calm after the storm
And ever vigilant for recurrence
Power of Nature over Man!

Morning Glory

Cold, bright, brilliant light
Silver frost settled unbroken.
The pond solid with packed ice.
Moorhens skating, looking for thaw
Fish unseen under the solid covering
Breath opaque as it touches the air.
Snowdrops pure against the sun.
The daffodils hang heavy with their burden.
The stillness of the morning
Uninterrupted.
Bird-like patterns unbroken by pressure
Everything carries calmness and tranquillity.
Relish the moment
It will pass
And the warmth of the day will break the spell.

Mary Ashton

I was born in a South Yorkshire village and lived most of my early life in Yorkshire. Nursing was my main line of work, but when I married my life changed (unfortunately we divorced some years later). My husband's work took us to many different towns and countries. We travelled from the north to the south of Africa, from the Sudan to Mozambique. We had many unforgettable experiences, from being caught up in the middle of the political coups, to the awesome view of Victoria Falls. I was treated like a lady, with servants waiting on my every whim. I attended a royal garden party with my husband and daughter, as well as travelling on a luxury cruise on the Atlantic. The other extreme was living in a garage with a corrugated iron roof, cooking meals and being a servant to others.

The contrasts in my life have given me a great sense of destiny and purpose. I can accept people without needing to know their background.

The wonderful thing about everything is, just as the bottom was about to fall out of my world, Jesus made Himself known to me. When I had almost given up, I received such wonderful hope. I accepted Jesus as my Lord and Saviour, and 'Behold, He made all things new'.

The experiences of this time are reflected in my poems. I had never written poetry before but now my heart and mind seemed so full of words and feelings, that I had to express them. I would wake up in the night and write a full poem, which I would read to my daughters the next day. The joy and peace were unexplainable. We still had very little, but somehow it didn't bother us anymore. We began to experience God's provision. Little things, big things, all kinds of miraculous interventions, just in time to save us.

The most exciting adventurous and joyous time was those early days of knowing Jesus. We know Jesus is real and is truly God. I think each person has a different introduction to Jesus according to their needs, which builds up a strong faith. You know that you know, even when you seem to be alone.

Each poem is the result of something special in my life; each poem has a story that borders on the impossible. When I relate my experiences, people may think I am making up a story to entertain them. Until they know Jesus they will never understand.

Thoughts In The Night

Dear Lord, I awake crying to you,
Dear Lord please tell me, what can I do?
Here I am Lord, I'm waiting, longing to know,
What can I do Lord, where can I go?
Here I am Lord, still waiting, asleep in my bed,
My throat now is aching, with words to be said,
Can I say 'I love you' in my own special way?
I want you to know Lord, how I'm feeling today,
I'm kneeling, I'm praying, I'm giving my all,
I hear you dear Father, I answer your call,
Dear Lord, my Master, my Saviour, my Friend,
I love you sweet Jesus,
This love has no end.

Surrender

There's a feeling of a nearness,
When I can see no one is there,
There's a warmth of love around me,
That makes me kneel in prayer,
How can you want me Jesus?
Why choose this life of mine?
My life is worthless rubbish,
There are better lives than mine.

Still I feel you, close beside me,
Your light is all around,
My heart can hear your loving words,
My ear yet hears no sound,
How can you love me Jesus?
My heart is made of stone,
I've learned to trust nobody,
I'll manage on my own.

And yet you stay beside me,
I'm tempted to give in,
Your loving hand to guide me,
Your blood frees me from sin,
I want to trust you Jesus,
Though my hope is very thin,
As I open up my heart's gate,
I feel all your love flow in.

Oh! My blessed glorious Saviour,
It's wonderful to know,
You can take a woman just like me,
And teach her, love can grow,
From a little tiny feeling,
Came this wonderful sensation,
From absolutely nothing,
Came this marvellous elation.

Teach me to be worthy,
My constant prayer will be,
Let me give God all the glory,
Let His love light shine through me.

Amen

Conversation

Here I am Lord, here I am,
What are you saying to me?
I try to push you aside but you won't let go,
What are you saying to me?

You demand my attention,
I can't understand which are your thoughts,
Which are mine,
What are you saying to me?

The day you first called me,
I wanted to go,
No matter where it would be,
Now I am waiting, longing to know,
What are you saying to me?

In my new life,
There's a deep love, a yearning,
A longing to do thy will,
Now I am burning, I'm waiting, I'm still,
Lord, what are you saying to me?

Thanks

Dear Lord, sweet Jesus,
As I kneel to pray,
I just want to say thanks for this glorious day,
I had a feeling,
With the first rays of light,
It would be one of those days,
Things would just turn out right,
And they did,
Thanks to you Lord,
It's so clearly true,
All things go right Lord,
When I'm trusting in you,
How great is my life, since I've learned,
Just to say,
I'm trusting in you Lord,
Then leave it that way,
Dear Lord, my sweet Jesus,
It's lovely to pray,
I love you and thanks,
It's a beautiful day.

Truth Is . . .

Is this really real?
Are all these strange happenings, happening to me?
Is this how I should feel?
Am I ready?
Is this how God wants me to be?
If I hadn't known,
If I hadn't been shown,
By now I would have presumed, it was all, imaginary.

But God touched me, I know,
It wasn't the kind of a feeling that I could invent,
It was a kind of a glow,
A magnetised feeling, I'm sure
It could only have been Heaven-sent,
I wanted to pray,
I wanted to say so many words,
But couldn't my body felt already spent.

Sometimes I think if I pinch myself, surely,
I would just come awake,
Sometimes I think,
I must be asleep and all that I need, is a really good shake,
But then I see you,
And then I see you,
So many people dreaming my dream,
That's too hard to take.

I feel in a trance,
The kind of sensation that makes me feel, I'm walking on air,
It's a slow motion dance,
My partner, a presence I feel, when nobody's there,
I say I love you,
He loves me too,
Then we move in rapture,
A mutual loving, without any care.

Thank God it's real,
This beautiful happiness,
Tranquil peacefulness, really is me,
Praise God, it's real,
This waiting knowingness, glorious glowingness,
Really is me,
I want to sing,
Praise to Jesus, my King,
Giving my life, giving my love, giving all,
As He wants it to be.

Love

Where did all this love come from?
I never had it before,
It began with a trickle,
Now it's a rush,
Like winter's ice, during spring thaw,
It began with a smile,
Then I added a song,
Now I'm wanting to dance all the time,
I feel like I just want to hug everybody,
And my words all come out in rhyme.

I know what happened,
I got to know Jesus,
I learned how He saved me from sin,
So I got baptised,
The water was lovely,
Now I want everyone to jump in,
I only have time to think thoughts about Jesus,
Look what's happened since I heard His name,
The old me died, I'm here resurrected,
With love, burning up like a flame.

Jesus now is my permanent lodger,
He's paid full price for his board,
The old me was kicked out,
I say 'Good riddance'
There's only rooms for my Lord!
He's taken me over,
I have no say,
He has cleansed all my rooms, free from sin,
Overnight I found, I'd stopped drinking and smoking,
I don't want any dirt to get in.

Let me tell you the secret,
The whole world can know,
The old me is waiting and still,
The new me is waiting, listening for Jesus,
Ready to move at His will,
Do you know what to do, to get some of this love?
It's for all, not just me, that He came,
Lift up both arms,
Call out, 'Jesus I need you,'
And for evermore just praise His name.

Walking In Love

Why are you weary my love, my friend?
What has caused you to frown,
With love I watch from a distance,
I see when your hands hang down,
You've drawn yourself away, alone,
Something hurting, your eyes have shown,
Something, maybe even to you, unknown,
Jesus told me to love you.

At times when you're weary my love, my friend,
There's always someone there,
There's always someone who sees you down,
And lifts you up on a prayer,
God hears the sound of the deepest sigh,
He knows the need and the angels fly,
It's not for us to question why,
Jesus told me to love you.

If ever you're weary my love, my friend,
Remember this special love,
Not the love of the world as the world knows love,
But direct from Heaven above,
This kind of love does not offend,
Love that wants to heal and mend,
Love that lays down His life for a friend,
Jesus told me to love you.

When you are weary my love, my friend,
Rest in the love that is there,
Try to remember, 'My burden is light,
My cross not too heavy to bear',
Draw yourself away, be still,
Quiet your mind and wait, until,
With the water of life, your cup He'll fill,
Jesus told me, He loves you.

Guess Who?

My love has a heart as big as a mountain,
My love is so gentle, so tender, so kind,
My love has a way of always just knowing,
What's in my heart, what's on my mind.

My love has a voice, loving and tender,
The sound brings me comfort when I'm in despair,
My love gives me peace, He knows just how to tell me,
Wherever I'm going, He'll always be there.

My love has a body to always protect me,
With His hands He constantly shows me His love,
When He stands beside me there's a tingle inside me,
My love is the kind of love dreams are made of.

Jesus has a heart as big as a mountain,
Jesus has a voice that is loving and kind,
Jesus gave of His body to always protect me,
Jesus' love is the purest love I'll ever find.

Jesus' love is so real I can almost touch it,
Jesus' love makes me tremble, the power is so strong,
When He stands beside me,
As this joy mounts inside me,
I whisper 'I love you' and sing a love song.

Jesus' love is so great, there is plenty left over,
God so loved the world that He gave us His Son,
When we sinned, He cried for us,
In our worst, He died for us,
Jesus' love is the greatest love sent from above.

I love him, I love him, I love him, I love him,
How else can I tell Him? What more can I say?
I will walk in His footsteps, I will be His disciple,
I will run the great race, I will try for the prize,
There's only one way I can be a disciple,
There will be Jesus' love for you lighting my eyes.

Better Late

It's never too late to know the Lord
It's never too late to hear His word
Our sins are forgiven, that's understood
The debt has been paid, by the price of His blood
He died on the cross our sins to relieve
Now all you have to do is believe
Read the Bible, hear in His word
It's never too late to know the Lord

Do you feel lost but you don't know why?
Do you feel so lonely, sometimes you could cry?
Do you feel empty, frustrated, down?
Do you feel you'd just like to get out of town?
Don't be discouraged, don't be misled
There was hope for Lazarus and he was dead
Read the Bible, hear in His word
It's never too late to know the Lord

He will be with you wherever you go
Just knock on His door and say hello
Tell Him your troubles
Tell Him your fears
Tell Him things you had bottled inside you
For years
As you tell Him, your heartache
He will relieve
Then you'll find it easy just to believe
Read the Bible, hear in His word
It's never too late to know the Lord.

Once you have repented before the Lord
Opened the Bible and heard His word
You'll find your life full
A glorious sensation
Everyone in church becomes a relation
You feel yourself cleansed
Your sins washed away
You'll see your old friends
And you'll hear yourself say,
'Read the Bible, hear in His word
It's never too late to know the Lord.'

Michael N Darvill

I know that in the beginning the world was perfect through the love of God. Everything God has ever done has been for us. He knows what's best for us. So He made Paradise and everything in it was good to perfection. Everything we did was good and to our liking. In this way God was pleased too and in our eyes God could do no wrong. Neither could we and we never did. The mind was kind to ourselves and each other. We saw everyone as equals. We were all as rich as one another. We never found fault with each other. We never felt threatened or hurt. There was no name-calling. We were always pleased and so contented. We wanted for nothing because we were happy with God and everything He had given us. We wanted for nothing more But God always gave us more love than before and with that love each of us gave more love to God. We trusted God with everything. We trusted God. Nothing could ever go wrong. The trust was lost so everything went wrong. God still loved us but we never returned that love. If we find love we will have that trust again to build a world fit for God and every one of us.

I tell you God is present. He is with us all and we must return the love to be like Him. We must be good, if you want to feel good - all you need is love. It's so simple and so powerful. The best things in life always are, Paradise world-wide and it's right here inside.

Life For Always

Shaken and stirred
No end to what's seen and heard.
Loud in a crowd
Or soft in the dust.
That's every one of us.
Coming and going,
Time always knowing.
Giving and taking,
Always creating,
More time for the waiting.
Life once again will come and remain.
Ashes from ashes,
Dust from the dust,
Life belongs to all of us.
And the Lord decides,
When to live,
And when to die.

A Promise Is A Promise

All day no end of play
Doing what I want of me.
Being myself.
A time to count my wealth.
And all my blessings.
All here together.
Never leaving.
Always receiving.
No end of believing
The truth.
I died
For you.
And here I stay
In myself this very day.
I will never leave you
Come what may.
You can rely on what I say.
I am for always.
OK.

The Present Time

The past can't come the past is dead
It can no longer raise its ugly head.
Gone and forgot.
For now is what we are.
The present time the best by far.
For everything happens now.
Everything always happens now.
Everything always happens now.
Everything has always happened now.
There's never been any other time but now.
So let happiness be yours and mine.
In this present time.

Wonderful You

Looking is not seeking.
Crying is not weeping.
Together we are sleeping.
All our hearts no longer apart.
No longer broken.
Familiar words never spoken.
All the peace.
Never again anything lame.
Just the power of love that's ours.
The family powers together forever.
Not hours.
A celebration in God's new nation.
God's creation.

Promise

I am as you and you are as me
One and the same we are everybody.
And nobody is to blame
We are all the same.
Everybody has the same soul.
It's me, I'm here, I am with thee.
I am God in everybody.
I am with you always.
The only sure way is always.
Together for always.
For my love is the sure way.
We will never be apart.
Because I have loved you from the start.
And there's no way we can part.
For everlasting is my art.
No death will us part.
A promise is a promise, nothing dishonest.
The faith is a promise.
Everlasting life honest.
The promise forever and ever.
Whichever longest.

Christ

For He took all.
All the sin that did dwell within
To give us life everlasting.
All the pain and the sorrow
Like there was no tomorrow
The collection of it all.
That was the day Christ was tall,
The biggest heart of us all.
And He remains the sacred one of all,
The living God,
The Lord so great and small,
The Saviour of us all
This very same day in the very same shroud
With the very same crowd.

Adam And Eve

There's no mistaking the mother and father of creating.
That's where we've been,
We are the making.
The family is still creating.
What a noise, and what a fuss
They make for all of us.
Living together would be a pleasure.
But the hell of it is their leisure.
Not at all learning to live together.
The teaching must be taught by the head of course.

Success Happiness

Barabbas set free,
God did not die needlessly.
He gave life to everybody.
Anyone missed?
No. All do live
It's life I give.
No end of this.
Again and again.
Until such a time
God says
You're mine.
The soul does need rest
And true happiness.
That's what God knows best.
Life and happiness you deserve.
I will be heard.
And you shall come
For you know you have won
A place with Father and Son.

Our Angels

Time so great. Gives and takes
In many ways for our sake.
The giving and taking in life
And in death.
Always for the best
And leaving what's left.
If death takes a child
Better it be for the child to be free.
For time gives a better place to live
For the child is more deserving,
That's what time gives.
Time is not wasteful.
There are better things for kids.
And if time gives. It's what's best.
Time does not waste anyone so great.
Time makes sure there is justice and more.
Better things like a pair of wings
Gabriel sings.

If Needs Be

Man needs time time does not need man.
Time does all it can and more
Time keeps score.
Every life is known for sure.
A time to come and a time to go.
The giving and taking
Time in the making.
Time knows how to give and take.
Time makes no mistake.
The biggest heart is the heart of time.
The heart of God.
As big as the swell of the sea
Metaphorically.

True Earnings

Sorry but still smiling.
Nothing of sorrow.
Smiling today
Still smiling tomorrow.
The God who gives to all that live
No end of truth.
What's truly meant for you
Is what's given it's true.
God knows sincerity and insincerity.
And what's truly meant is God-sent.
What's truly earned is what's truly got.
Be patient you'll have the lot.
Just like God.

God The Provider, A Familiar Sight

We all have a need to be part of the family
And the family of God is the one for me.
Charity begins at home,
For my Father knows.
He's always telling me so.
Everywhere I see,
It's charity for you and charity for me.
Throughout our lives
It's the God in you and the God in me
Providing for everybody:
The family of God pulling together
Through love.
I am proud to be part of my family
And proud of my Father,
The Provider.
Because when I fall. He's always there
And when I call. Everyone helps me
One and all.

Inside Alive

Here it comes
Paradise, I am the one.
The one God
Your true love.
I am there with you, it's understood
Paradise will come through love.
Peace is good
It does what it should.
I am God, your love.
Your good self in all of us.
The goodness in you,
The goodness in me,
Yes. Your neighbour.
The goodness you see in yourself
Your true wealth
Your paradise is thee.
Don't despair.
Practice will give you the life within you.
Heaven will begin within.
In paradise there's no sin.

My Adored Ways

Heaven adored, praise be to the Lord.
He's exceptional for sure.
He's Heaven and always more.
Always greater than before.
Cometh unto the Father
He is happiness forever after.
Always great and full of laughter.
Giving fun to everyone who does come.
My will be done.
Happiness for everyone.
No one forgotten.
My ways are my ways.
Always sure ways.
Through my doorway.
All ways are sure ways.
No wrong in anyone.
The past has gone.
Only what belongs has come.
The sin, no memory of him.
Praise be to the King.

Good And Loving

The Lord God is my best friend
And He's with me till the end.
That's when He takes me to the top
For all my trouble and bad luck.
Because He knows I really tried
To help my neighbour by my side,
And all those who did pass by.
For I heard their human cry.
As I hear the Lord say.
Try to be good and loving
And you will succeed if you listen to me.

Peace For Oneself

Be good to the one you're with
And your rewards will be of enormities.
Wealth beyond wealth, friendship beyond self.
Happiness beyond, but now found.
No longer for what you long.
A world for each and everyone.
A world for father, mother, daughter and son.
The entire family as is we, the family of God.
Begging to be loved, wanting that special world.

Let's build it for every boy and girl.
Let's build it for oneself.
For we are all one and the same.
No matter what creed or name.

I am as you and you are as me.
A human being who needs love and security.
Being good to the ones you're with,
Will keep you and treat you
As if we are one.

Be good to the one you're with as if it's yourself.
And into peace we will be released.
And all misdemeanours will cease.

R P Scannell

My employment with the flow and meaning of words placed together to create a picture in one's thoughts. This gift I believe started from my early days at school. I remember one teacher, an English master by the name of John Dilger, a kind and yet a strong man who was involved in the First World War conflicts. He would make visits to parent that had been taken ill, in his own time. He also enjoyed reading the thoughts of W H Davies, known as the supper tramp. It was a real pleasure to one's ears. After school years, I had an illness that lasted a year and a half. In hospital, I was left with plenty of spare passing time. I was then, and today, fond of bible reading, and would try to put pen to paper.

Over the years I have been interviewed by local press, have received letters from the Queen's office, and also the owner-then of Harrods of London. The reason - my poem published about the Princess of Wales.

Whenever out and about, I do use my gift of sight to see nature's endless wonders, and value the seasons' changing ways. I do enjoy the silent ways of Mother Nature who has no need or use of boasting ways, (unlike us human beings - we seem to have a need). My poems hold a true value for me - from a smile on a face, a kind spoken word, and yet again my poems can relate to the ongoing problems of the world. My wish is to be able, with the gift of sight, to continue to observe and place my own thoughts down, and whenever possible, to share them with others in the passing life on Earth.

Layers Of Colour

Layers of colour - is the sky in sight -
filling my mind and eyes with delight -
this time of the day - making ready to
meet the night - whatever the speed or
pace of this life - that can take our thoughts
far away - always remember to stop -
and look - for the time of the day that
makes ready - to surrender to the night.

Poor Man's Wine - Water

When days are warm - and my throat is dry -
my mind turns to a poor man's wine -
no greater taste - on this Earth -
than that first drink to quench your thirst.

My Hidden Praise

I never knew her - we never spoke a word
now she is far, far away - still her thoughts and ways
are very close to me - I understand her endless
kindness - for the other living souls on the Earth
and she was blessed by Heaven's hand
with natural beauty and fine grace.
Was she an angel? - No,
she was known by the name of
Diana, Princess of Wales.
    Amen

`Har-Megedon´ - The Hebrew Name

I wonder - are there other human souls like me
Wondering when the heavens' war will begin?
When she has to pour out her just anger
Against the wicked nations on this Earth.
A time when the book on all suffering -
Pain that visits the body and mind
A time indeed when no one on the Earth
Will say they are sick or in any kind of pain.
The war of Heaven will bring in
Years and years of lasting peace -
Man on Earth will learn war no more.
First must come the anger
That has been up to now contained
Right up to this very day.
No one left on planet Earth will ever be heard to say
That Heaven in her wisdom
Never allowed enough time
For mankind to change his wicked ways.
That wouldn't be true -
Time enough has passed by
Bells of truth still ring out both loud and clear
Letting all mankind understand the will of God
Will be carried out.
No force of powers at that time will be able to stand
They will be brushed aside by Heaven's might hands
And just will be the act.
Heaven has a wisdom that is always fair
Taking into account all points of view
Before she acts - and act she will.
Man on Earth has been on notice for a long, long time.
His days are short and a name has been chosen
For the war of wars - known in Hebrew
As 'Har Magedon', the last war of them all
Come Lord Jesus - come quickly.
  Amen

Beauty

Beauty has no gains to play
When death near at hand
A loved one lost
Then one must learn to live alone?
Now at this late hour
Beauty has no ring
Yet dreams stay with us to the end
Making beauty just a friend.

Weeping Willow Trees By The Hogsmill River

The wonder of the weeping willow so big and tall
with branches like long arms hanging low -
I look and see you are ready to meet an endless flowing stream -
your cover of leaves come and disappear as the seasons change -
leaving the water to flow endlessly on its never-ending quiet quest
to reach the open sea.

The Christ - The Man

We have joy, we have peace - that time of year is with us once again -
when we are asked to remember the man - the Christ -
the greatest man who ever lived on planet Earth -
He was and is the only one that can, in truth offer everlasting life
to man on Earth - even if a man dies - he can live again -
by the powers of the Christ - we have joy, we have peace -
the Christ will come again without a doubt.
Amen

The Story Of A Tiny Seed!

With tender thoughts - and caring hands -
a tiny seed was planted in the earth -
there to rest and sleep - then with the passing
days of life - that tiny seed came to life -
started to show that wonder by appearing
above the earth - now with the powers of the sun -
and the light of day - that tiny seed started to gain
a strength within itself - now full-grown is
known to all - seeking eyes as a flower of beauty -
that in turn will bless our gift of sight.
Amen

A Thunderstorm

Can it be God above is angry with mankind?
Looking down He sees a world -
where man is killing man - with no end in sight -
hate and unkindness seem a way of life.

Can it be now and again God's anger is shown
by a thunderstorm - telling mankind -
He is well aware of what is going on -
still showing His loving kindness to the world.

How long will the one that dwells alone
hold back His judgement day? Will mankind
decide to make a needed change, or will a thunderstorm
from the heavens bring an end to mankind?
Amen

That Time Of Year Again

The long hours of winter days - and early nights -
have given way to new days of spring - bringing with them
new life, new growth to nature's ways on Earth.
Trees now in full leaf while butterflies dance in fields of green,
together with white daisies and yellow buttercups.
New days of creation's ways that give us a reason to look
at her works of art. From bluebells hidden in a quiet wood,
to young spring lambs dancing in green fields.
A wondrous time is this time of year, again.
Amen

The Arrangement

From times beginning to our days' decline -
man has gone from bad to worse - not knowing
how to find a way that leads to peace and joy -
no misunderstanding reason should lead man into fear -
he should be able to look to a future - bright and clear -
clear to plan and build on things that will not pass
man was meant to live -not fade away like summer grass.

Autumn's Carpet

That third season in a passing year has arrived - again
when nature's falling leaves - are forming a carpet at our feet,
a last act from nature's summer -
leaves - that have turned gold
still holding the power to catch our gift of sight
and to the last - there is a pleasure
of autumn's carpet - waiting at our feet.

Paved With Gold - Is London Town

Paved with gold - I have been told - is London town
grand hotels - well-tended parks - to laze around
kings and queens in palaces have lived there -
and still do - to this very day
fine shops - with all kinds of goods to delight
and shows - put on at night to entertain
sad to say - there are other sights
people using the street pavement
to lay down their heads to sleep at night -
for whatever reason - and I am not a judge.
Yes, two stories can be told of London town -
one with its streets paved with gold -
and one with a body - sleeping out in the cold!

War And Leaves

With all the wars that mankind made
what a waste of pain that labour brings
lives lay lost and reasons fade - mankind
it seems is unable to reason without a fight -
lives are lost - leaving the bloodstains
hidden by the earth - yet seen by Heaven high -
in contrast, the leaves that fall from the trees
do more good and help bring life anew -
man must learn war, no more -
mankind must look to God to unite.

Time And Tide

The grass, they say - in the wisdom of this world -
Is always green on the other side
How true to this life - mankind always comparing what he is
What he has - to enjoy the glory of his world
Sad to say that also the saying is true
Time and tide wait for no man on this Earth
He grows old - his days of life come to an end
Till Heaven is no more - he must sleep in death
Until the powers of Heaven recall all that have fallen
To the powers of death - when they can look to a future bright
With grass that is forever green - to endless time
With days of joy - happening on a paradise Earth.
    Amen

When I Leave

What honest values can I leave - when I must leave the world behind?
A few moments of careful thoughts pass - and then the answer
comes to me - my book of poems put together over the
passing years - I will leave for searching eyes -
to read with ease my thoughts - written down - they will know -
I was blessed to see new buds of spring turn into full leaf -
that my gift of sight was used to search the ever-changing skies -
and I was blessed many times by moments of real peace -
all from Mother Nature's creative works of art.
    Amen

Please Judge Me Lord!

I have loved - the dwelling of your house - and I will sing
your praises throughout the land - as for me - in my integrity -
I shall walk, and I shall walk around your altar grand -
then judge me Lord - my Jehovah God - in you I trust -
I don't trust the hands of man - that are full of bribes -
and I have loved the dwelling of your house - your temple -
all so grand - and I will march around your altar grand -
giving thanksgiving throughout the land.
     Amen

In My Need!

In my need - I am searching everywhere
I search my very soul in my need to care
by word of mouth I make my request
to the heights of Heaven's ways -
bless me with continued faith -
to make it through each day of life -
that when I have a need of a close friend -
you will be that one to comfort me -
let me understand - that by faith
I can draw close to you - no demands you make -
I have a choice to believe and trust in you -
or be as one that has no hope -
from day to day in life - now in my closing thought -
I pray you above - are never far away from me.
     Amen

Understanding

Your Earth - and the ways they work - are beautiful -
Please help us to be able to understand - understand
your will on Earth be done - help me to see the rains
from Heaven - bringing freshness to your Earth -
please help us trust your mighty hands - let me turn away from
hands of greedy man. Let me see your bright tomorrow -
ending all the Earth's tears that follow sorrow - let me
trust you alone - to bring us back to your great love -
a love without ending for everyone - everyone that loves
your way and would - then ask for your will on Earth -
to be done.

A Request

Dear friend - when in doubt put faith and all
your trust in Jehovah God - his thoughts and powers
far outreach that of any man on Earth - faith is not blind -
faith requests your trust - and with that trust -
a pathway to happiness - you have placed in our God above.

Sarah Auld

I am a twenty-seven-year-old New Zealander who currently lives in the United Kingdom with my husband.

I grew up as part of a Christian family in a rural community in the very south of New Zealand. My family was very active in every way, they were heavily involved in the local church, sports teams, school boards and many other community commitments.

When I was eighteen I left home to study physiotherapy in Auckland (the big smoke in the far north), as it had always been my dream to become a physio. In my second year at Physiotherapy School, I became seriously ill with what was later diagnosed as chronic fatigue syndrome. This was an extremely trying time for me as it shook my world to its roots. Sport, study, church commitments and a busy social life had been what I had grown up with and what I thrived on. Suddenly all this was taken from me. It forced upon me a real time of growth as a Christian because, for the first time in my life, I faced the decision of whether I would still worship God when it seemed that He offered me no blessings.

It has been eight years since I first become ill with chronic fatigue syndrome and it is an ongoing battle to manage my health. Throughout this time I have found the restrictions and difficulties forced upon me an amazing blessing in my relationship to God. It has forced me to be real in my faith, honest with God, honest with myself and honest with those around me. It has brought out in me the gift of writing poetry and developed in me many traits I would never have been aware of if it wasn't for my sickness.

My first book entitled, 'A Collection Of Thoughts' will be published at the end of this year.

Who Am I?

I am a child of God, a servant of His
I am heir to His kingdom, co-heir with Christ
I am daughter of the Almighty King, and sister of Christ the Messiah
I am wife to the man I love, part of a lifelong union
I am the recipient of love and commitment, and giver of that also
I am daughter and sister of a wonderful family, loved and accepted
    and always valued
I am a physio, a health professional who seeks to heal, advise,
    enable and help
I am a sufferer of ME, whose activity is limited by my health
    and whose every day is governed by how I feel
But it is not my marriage or my family or my job or my sickness
    that defines me
It is God living in me
Moulding, changing, forgiving and loving me
That makes me who I am
For always, above all else, I am a child of God.

Sickness Teachers

I used to mock picky eaters
    I'm now on a gluten-free, wheat-free, dairy-free diet
I used to mock vegetarians,
    I no longer eat red meat.

I used to look down on people who walk to get fit,
    Now walking is my only means of fitness
I used to look down on people who don't exercise,
    For periods of many months I can do nothing but rest.

I used to think it was weak to limit your activity
Because you were busy or tired,
    Now I know the foolishness of not
I used to think only weak people got depression,
    I was on anti-depressants for ten months.

I used to think being busy was the only way to a productive life,
    I now know the amazing value of having time to sit
    With friends, meditate on God's word and pray for as
    Long as I need to.

I used to think my friendships depended on what I could put
Into them,
    I now know the joy of being loved and accepted even
    When I have nothing to offer.

I used to think I could do anything I wanted,
    I now know I have limitations.
I used to think 'experiences' were so important,
    I now know only God and people matter.

Sickness has taught so much about what to value,
And so much about what to discard.
Funny how God works - isn't it?

Answers

Lord, sometimes I despair with medicine
After generations of study
We still know so little
Why does no one know what is wrong with me?
No one can explain to me
    why my body tires so easily
    and my muscles ache with so little exertion

Lord I know that You know
You are my Creator
My Healer
My Doctor
You know my body
And You know the answers
Why don't You explain to me
    why my body tires so easily
    and my muscles ache with so little exertion?

Lord, I feel that my body has failed me
It's not doing the job it was designed for
Food that is supposed to nourish, damages
Exercise that is supposed to strengthen, weakens

Why did You give me a body that fails so often?

Maybe You know that a weak body will strengthen my desire for You
Maybe You see how physical failure will give me spiritual hunger
Maybe my body hasn't failed me
Maybe it's doing exactly what You intended
Maybe You know me better than I do
Maybe I'll leave the answers with You

Deep Hurts

Exhaustion: crippling, disabling, limiting
It cancels my plans, stops my activity, changes my lifestyle
It makes work a struggle and my leisure hard to enjoy
It makes minuscule tasks mountainous and small problems massive
It forces me to stop
It commands me to rest or face the consequences
It changes who I am
I can no longer do
No church commitments, no sport,
No full-time occupation, no busy social schedule
I'm forced to rest
To stop activity
To be still

No busy schedule to keep my mind from deeper things
From doubts I don't want to voice
From hurts I don't want to feel
From fears I don't want to face
No activity to protect me from the wounds of my heart
Just hours of stillness to think about them
I can't ignore them
I can't hide from them
I can't bury them
Mistakes I keep reliving
Hurtful comments I keep feeling
Failures I keep replaying
The hurt overwhelms me

But quietly
Standing next to me
God is waiting
To take these hurts from me
To heal me from them completely
He forces me to face them
He takes away everything I hide behind
He exposes my deep hurts
Then He takes my wounds
And He heals them

Humbled

I'm being humbled
I'm being brought low
Broken
Crushed
Dismantled
No pride to cling to
No achievements to boast about
No strength to rely on
Having to admit the extent of my weakness
Needing to ask for help
Admitting I can't cope
Allowing others to see my hurt and my faults

It's so hard being humbled
I want to be strong
I want to cope
To be independent
To be known for my strength not my weakness
To be able to give rather than forced to receive
To earn my worth, to contribute my share, to prove my value
I don't want to be humbled
I want to be proud
To shine with strength
To achieve great things
To make a difference
To have an impact
To change what is not right
To help the weak
Not to be weak

I want to be strong
To be healthy and fit, busy and active
To be emotionally strong, full of joy and laughter
To be bubbly and energetic, caring and giving
To be unselfish and thoughtful, aware of others' needs
Not dominated by my own

122

But God wants other things
He chooses to make me weak
And limit my physical abilities
He gives me hurts I need help to deal with
And forces me to rely on Him and others
God wants me to be weak

Striving

Striving
Trying hard
Giving lots
Serving others
Doing our best

Striving for righteousness
Earning our purity
Being nice
Being good
No nasty words
No impure thoughts
No sins

It doesn't work
We can't get there
We'll never reach God's mark
Our efforts are pitiful
Our purity, filthy

But there is a way
God's purity
His sacrifice
His forgiveness
His cleansing
For us

Our future secured
By His grace

Naked

Our hearts, souls and minds, naked before Him
That is what our Heavenly Father desires
No hidden areas
No clothing of protection
No wall of defence
Just us, open to Him

He's seen our hearts naked
It doesn't embarrass Him
It doesn't disgust Him
When we come to Him naked, He is filled with love for us
No matter how our heart looks, it is beautiful to Him
Because it is our gift to Him

He knows us intimately
He created us, and He knows what we have become
We have no need to hide ourselves from Him
He wants us to bare our souls to Him
To lay our hearts openly before Him
To reveal to Him all that is on our mind

We need to go to our Heavenly Father
With our hearts, minds and souls naked before Him
Let's strip ourselves of our defences
Let's uncover the areas that we hide
Let's give ourselves to our Heavenly Father
For that is what He desires

Anxious

Does God ever consider our problems
    too insignificant to deal with or
    to complicated to bother with?

Did Jesus care about the little things?
Well He performed a miracle to feed thousands
People that weren't starving
    that hadn't gone without food for days
    that weren't going to die if they missed this meal
People that simply had missed out on lunch
    because they were listening to Jesus

So He fed them
Not for a week or a month
Not for the rest of their lives
But just for that moment
Because they were hungry and in need
Because He cared

Jesus cares about our problems
He cares about the little things
He cares about whatever concerns us
    and disturbs the peace He intends for us

Jesus cares
And while He may not always intervene
He loves, He supports, He guides
And from time to time, He performs miracles

The Joy Of Knowing The Lord

Having happiness that doesn't depend on circumstances
Knowing a love that doesn't depend on our efforts
Trusting in someone who we know is in complete control
Being able to give our problems to the Ruler of all
Experiencing God's goodness in the midst of suffering
Feeling valued, even when we have nothing to offer
Giving praise to a pure, perfect and holy God
Knowing our future doesn't depend on our abilities
Feeling forgiven, loved and accepted
And knowing we always will be

Heavenly Eyes

Lord give me Heavenly eyes
That I might see hearts, not bodies
See needs, not weaknesses
See hopes, not faults
That I would love and not judge
Forgive and not remember
Help and not count the cost

Lord I want to be like you
I want to have eyes like you
Take from me my sight
That looks at bodies and fashions and faces and professions
That sees faults and weaknesses and mistakes
Give me your sight Lord
That looks at hearts
That sees need
That loves

Lord in my earthly body
I want to have Heavenly eyes

Humility

Humility
Humbleness
Jesus

Washing feet
Accepting abuse
Forgiving friends
Loving a traitor
Having nothing
Giving everything
Wanting no glory
Except for the Father

Humility
Humbleness
Jesus

Stuart Plumley

 Stuart Plumley was born in Central India where his father was working among the Tribal Gonds of Bastar State in the jungle village of Narainpur. At the age of five he went to boarding schools in the Himalayas where he spent nine months of the year for over thirteen years. He was twenty when he realised he had been on the wrong course, but first served nearly five years in the army.

In February 1947 he came to England to study with The London School of Journalism. It was a relief that learning was not difficult as with science, but it meant a reorientation and re-education.

He began with articles, completed two novels and then a play. On 17th February 1967, he won second prize from over fifty entries in the Borough of Barnet's play-writing competition. He sent his plays to theatres with encouraging responses.

Suddenly he began writing poetry. Greatly excited, he completed a long narrative poem, then *The Village Fool,* a three-act verse play; about a dozen lyrics and thought out the tunes. An Irish singer borrowed 'Samantha' as a signature tune, well-received in night clubs.

The Black Rock, a children's novel, was accepted by the BBC. At their request he adapted it to a radio play of ten episodes. The first three were broadcast. Radio 5 took over and decided teachers did not like animals being killed. He wrote the abridgement of Anita Desai's novel, *Village by the Sea,* hoping to be given the serialisation for radio and television, but was poached by another producer. More radio and television plays were written and then a historical novel.

The International Society of Poets nominated him 'Poet of the Year' for four years, inviting him to Washington, Florida, Hollywood, and then Washington. His work was included in special editions of selected poems and he has had several poems published by *Poetry Now.*

The Exile

Sometimes when riding in a train or bus,
I see in London, or in some such place,
A tree, an ancient car, or just a thrush
And in a trice I have a younger face.
My burdens lift and I remember the days
I lived so near the Indravati's flow,
And knew so well the life of jungle ways,
Then studied beneath the peaks of frozen snow.

The road is red and through the jungle snakes:
My mother by my father's side will speak
Of home, the joys and cares she undertakes
While her three sons doze off to the body's creak.
Security! It's great that one belongs
To state and home with play in all those suns!
To morning dew and jungles filled with songs!
To tanks, waterfalls, rivers and our guns!

The Indravati river's bridge is wide
And tells us we'll be home in a moment's time.
The barking dogs remind us where they're tied.
Let lose they dance about with joy sublime,
Their barks and capers making us replete
For through nine months they've not forgotten us
As friskily they scamper round our feet.
Oh dogs! You dogs! What joy was in your fuss!

The bright sun shone and tall trees cast cool shades
Along the paths I trod in the jungle's green.
I saw the gentle cheetal in the glades,
The whistlers in the reeds, the parrots preen,
The snipe beside the water's edge, and bright
Green pigeons hiding in the pipal trees.
I saw the birds and beasts in sudden flight
Which told me of the jungle's mysteries.

The sparks that crackled from within the wood
Contented grunts from men the silence boosts.
The naked Gonds enhanced all that was good,
While peacocks called aloud from jungle roosts.
A lonely cheetal's cry then rent the air
As from a village hut the drumbeats throb.
A tiger's rumbling voice said, 'Now beware!'
As the jungle darkened round the lighted blob.

I rose at dawn to wander with my gun
And rifle through the jungle tracks and found
The game abound before the rising sun
When morning mists rose and dew lay on the ground.
What matters if I return with an empty hand
When verdant land around me blest my path
And jungle noises made a pleasant band
Which music even now is close to my heart?

I talk of friends, both dark of face and white,
Who smiled in friendship and who knew my heart
And soul belonged to jungle birds in flight
And graceful antlered deer, so proud, who dart
In leaping fear through jungles thick with trees.
The panthers' and the tigers' master stand
Whose muscled graceful actions all men please.
These were the things I had to understand.

I wore no satchel on my way to schools:
Ensconced beneath Himalayan peaks I trod
The road to knowledge and despising fools
I learnt to play and rough with other gods
And so for manhood knew just where I stood,
For I had friends, companions and those things
To make us one of many: understood
And more acceptable as human beings.

But gloating time will change the path we tread
And through the years it laughed at my own plight.
Now friends and comrades round the globe have spread,
Forgotten shadows of a world in flight.
Nor can my closest roam the jungles known
By us and ours, for life has dealt its shafts
Of cruel arrows and I would walk alone,
A spared but no wiser man in wisdom's rafts.

I think of servants, pets and bullock carts,
Of men and women bearing heavy loads
While soothing sunshine warmed their simple hearts.
I see the people walking on the roads
With friendly smiles because they knew my youth,
They were my life, a life of simplicity,
Where men and women never seemed uncouth,
But bore an aura of amiability.

But now I see my children welcome home
A balding, ageing man who must be wise.
Excitedly they hang onto these bones
And when I look into their shining eyes,
I know I'm loved because of what belongs
To them and theirs and all that they have loved.
My rose, my dahlias and my raucous songs
Will be to them, in time, as all I loved.

You'll Never Grow Old

Torrential rain falls in a land that is harsh,
Where the wind blows so fiercely it whips at the earth,
Where the crops fail the people year after year,
Where the children are old from the time of their birth.
There sits a mother deeply concerned
For the child in her arms who people have spurned,
And she coos and she sighs at those stark staring eyes
While she tries to console the child as it dies.
'You'll never grow old my babe,
You'll never grow old.
Your bones won't be brittle,
You won't feel the cold.'

God gave us this land at the time we were born,
We loved it as those in more fortunate climes.
We built and we ploughed as our fathers before,
We loved and we toiled as we did at all times.
We laughed and we cried when the day's work was done
And contentedly lived beneath a fierce sun.
Then the elements ravaged and lay waste our homes,
There was nothing to do but bury our bones.
'You'll never grow old my babe,
You'll never grow old.
Your bones won't be brittle,
You won't feel the cold.'

Oh don't look at me with your dear trusting eyes,
Enormous and pleading which must be in vain.
It's the sun and the wind that rules all our lives,
Though people will say it's our fault that we're slain.
The young girl laid herself down for a rest
And a whirlwind of dust stirred the rags which were best.

In a land where there's plenty and food's thrown away
The people are asking for more every day.
'You'll never grow old my babe,
You'll never grow old.
Your bones won't be brittle,
You won't feel the cold.'

The Muria's Song Of The Jungle

Dawn will whisper in the day,
Then the cocks will crow away.
Peacocks call to rouse us all,
Day breaks and the jungles call.
Dew is silver on the grass,
While the cobwebs form white lace.
Birds will cheer me as I pass
And the trees with shade embrace.
This is home, my jungle home, a Muria's home

See the sunshine through the trees,
See the cheetal as they freeze,
See the does alert for foes,
And the proud stag's antlered woes.
Numerous are the friendly streams
Trickling through the plains and hills,
Gentle valleys as man dreams,
That my heart much joy fulfils.
This is home, my jungle home, a Muria's home.

Night beneath a diamond sky,
Fires crackle, people sigh.
Drums will beat from wild retreats,
Rolls the tiger's rumbling beats.
So beside the fire's glow
Friends will smile, love overflow,
While the citadel of trees
Whisper softly in the breeze.
This is home, my jungle home, a Muria's home

A Muria's Lament For His Love

My love lies in the jungle's depth
And tears, so like the Indravati, flow
From eyes tormented red by a grieving soul.
Here lofty trees looked down upon our play,
Their prying eyes a witness to a shared
Encounter, fluid, gentle, kind and warm;
Then jungle fires set alight desires
To leave charred remnants to enrich the soil.

Her sighs were those of a gentle whispering stream,
Her flowing fingers gliding like a snake
Brought raptures such as makes a peacock dance.
A peacock I was and strutted for her charms,
So joyful that the monkeys and the birds
Sang praises in the trees above our heads:
The hard bare ground became a feather bed
And so we floated to the highest peaks.

My love was dancing naked just for me
The sun shining softly through shadowing trees
Adored a face and figure and a smile
Of roguish fun and beauty - celestial fired.
My love sighed as she fell dead at my feet
And I watched a large beast spirit her away,
Too petrified to help or even speak.
I was afraid, unable to move my limbs.

My love was loved by me within this glade,
Her soft flesh answering all my whims.
A tiger ravished her in his own way
And jungle scavengers scattered her remains.
Now every day her spirit beckons me
To mock the coward who remained unmoved,
Because a terror all his limbs had seized.
. . . My love lies in the jungle, where lies my love?

A Muria Lament - The Black Rock

(In memory of the real lovers portrayed in my novel)

Let the drumbeats throb in lamentation,
Let the bells be mute because we're weeping,
Let our songs proclaim our adulation,
Let us tell a tale enriched by loving.
God gave gifts of laughter, love and lustre,
Which enhanced our joys in all our actions,
Luminous and radiant with good humour,
Because their smiles would dissipate all factions.

Let the rivers flood by women keening,
Let the jackal's raillery pain harrow,
Let the peacock's dance be one of mourning,
Let the monkey's chatter cease with sorrow
Penda and Karingo loved with passion,
Danced abandoned in their joy of living,
Brother and sister to every person,
Thus to embrace all in their joy of giving.

Let their beauty be remembered by us,
Let their final act of love be honoured,
Let their joyful hearts become illustrious,
Let us sing a song to last forever.
Lie you lovers in a grave together
As another world awaits your spirits.
We will grieve and yet a richness savour,
When we see those stones where you lie buried.

*This is to commemorate the real lovers, a young husband and wife.
The wife was taken by a man-eater, the husband followed the trail and
killed it with his spear though he himself was mauled to death. The
episode was described to me by Norval Mitchell, an administrator with
whom I spent many pleasant outings in Bastar.*

Scenes From Childhood - `Grandfather´

He sat on the verandah:
The transparent parchment skin of his face
Criss-crossed by thin red veins.
Lack-lustre blue eyes gazed vacantly,
Seeing nothing but the womb from whence he had come.
Time trembled through the tropical torpor - backwards:
The vale of Gardano stretched before him,
The antennae of ancestral auras affixed.
He wandered through the paths of boyhood,
The hills he had climbed across the valley,
The pathways leading through the luscious fields,
The Cross Tree standing by the village centre,
The church where all his family worshipped.

These things were real:
His mother calling him to her bosom.
All else was unreal:
Parading on numerous barrack squares,
Marriage and a self-inflicted exile,
Grandsons on whom he gazed with amused indifference,
The men he protected from marauding tigers,
Or the innocent from those who were precocious,
Serving God and building for his purpose,
Being unemployed because the mission was Americanised,
Then a new life in the densest jungles,
His rightness and rectitude revealed as life was simple,
Truth tenacious, tranquil and transcendental,
All forgotten as his spirit journeyed
Back to his birth and the new awakening.

The Office Dance

Sweet Laura with the Mona Lisa smile,
Alone and wistful, swaying in a dance,
Her secrets locked in an enigmatic style,
That made an old man take his chance.

Sweet Laura smiled and danced so winsomely,
It charmed the old man to his heroic days,
The days he had frolicked in an endless spree,
And many beautiful girls would sing his praise.

Sweet Laura soon beheld a young man's charms,
And in a flash she dashed the old man's ego.
She fled and nestled in those youthful arms
And left the old man nursing his lumbago.

The old man looked at Laura's shining face,
Her teeth laid bare as a mare's before it neighs,
Ecstatic in her pleasure and the chase
To flirt with the young in a young girl's ways.

The old man laughed at the girl's perfidy,
The right was hers to exercise her win.
Then through his wisdom and his folly,
Eureka!
He found what made the Mona Lisa grin.

Keith C L Ball

I am a retired schoolteacher and I live in the village of Codsall, South Staffs, on the outskirts of Wolverhampton, where I have lived since 1959. Before that I lived in Fallings Park, Wolverhampton. I am married to Hazel and have two children, Elizabeth and Nicholas, who are both married. Nicholas lives nearby in Bilbrook and Elizabeth lives in Rawlins, Wyoming, USA. I have two grandsons, Nicholas and Joshua.

Although Codsall has grown somewhat since 1959, it still is a very pleasant place in which to live. The beautiful church of St Nicholas was built some 900 years ago and overlooks the village from the brow of a hill and the surrounding countryside contains many areas of outstanding beauty.

I have always been particularly interested in the written word, whether poetry or prose and am an avid reader.

I have written a book about Wyoming, past and present, and this was dedicated to my two grandchildren. It has not as yet been published but I live in hope that perhaps some day it might.

I am sure that my love of writing and poetry stemmed from my education at Wolverhampton Grammar School, where I had the opportunity to study outstanding works of literature and poetry.

Since my retirement, I have found the time to pursue my interests and I intend to continue writing about things which inspire me to do so.

The Wye Valley

When thinking of an area,
Where I might spend a day,
The valley of the River Wye,
Is where I love to stay.

To Ludlow then to Leominster,
And when I've passed them by,
I reach the place I'm looking for,
The beautiful valley of the Wye.

I stopped a while at Weobley,
Unique in every way,
There is a charming coffee shop,
Where I just love to stay.

A walk around the village,
The buildings, black and white,
A lovely church to visit,
The place is a delight.

Then on to lovely Eardisland,
A village beyond compare,
The charming River Arrow,
Adds to the beauty there.

There is a sense of timelessness,
As I wander through the place,
It's typical of England past,
Perhaps one last embrace.

I stopped for lunch at the local pub,
Then on the road once more,
This time heading for Hay-on-Wye,
Lots of books to explore.

It was a market day in Hay,
The folks were milling round,
For many people came to look,
And some to spend a pound.

When I left Hay, I journeyed on,
To Ross-on-Wye at last,
And after that to Symonds Yat
The view is unsurpassed.

I turned for home soon after,
And in my mind I stored,
An area of the country,
One that I adored.

January

The New Year brings us ice and snow,
Long lines of traffic, moving slow,
But gradually the roads are clear,
Not an auspicious start to the year.

Children travelling home from school,
Snowball fights by the frozen pool,
The street lamps' glow will light their way,
At closing of a winter's day.

A hoar frost settles throughout the night,
Come morning, an amazing sight,
A masterpiece of winter born,
To grace a January morn.

February

The ice began to melt today,
I dearly hope it stays that way.
The weatherman says rain is due,
I trust that what he says is true.

And sure enough the following day,
The rain washed all the ice away.
It was a joy to walk once more,
Instead of sliding to the floor!

The days move on, young shoots appear,
It happens at this time of year,
For spring is waiting close at hand,
To take its place throughout the land.

March

A sense of joy is close at hand,
As March winds sweep across the land,
And trees are buffeted to and fro,
Wherever you may care to go.

The strolls along the country lanes,
It never matters if it rains,
A stunning view, beyond compare,
New life is beginning everywhere.

Daffodils, tulips and hyacinths too,
In full array, a wonderful view,
The sun breaks through, a shower to follow,
And circling above, the very first swallow.

April

This month of blustery winds and showers,
Is blessed with many lovely flowers,
While sitting and enjoying them all,
I'm sure I heard a cuckoo call!

And when we come to Easter Day,
With all the eggs out on display,
A lovely sight beyond compare,
No wonder we just stand and stare.

Each day that passes the sun is higher,
Like some gigantic ball of fire,
Sustaining us with warmth and light,
From early morn to latest night.

May

The gardens are looking bright and gay,
With springtime flowers in full array.
The latest frosts have now gone, I hear,
I wish it could stay like this all year.

Summer is only a short step away,
And fledglings appear almost every day.
Not yet full grown, they bask in the sun,
Their parents' work now almost done.

The colourful blossom is thick on the trees,
The scent of the hawthorn wafts on the breeze,
It matters little, whether red or white,
Its perfume is with us day and night.

June

The long and balmy days are here,
It is a lovely time of year,
To sit outdoors, admiring the view,
Is something that we love to do.

The new-mown lawns, so fresh and green,
Look better than they've ever been,
And flowering plants enhance the view,
Roses, pinks, clematis too.

Midsummer Day is almost here,
The twenty-fourth of June, my dear,
And when it's come and been and gone,
The days grow shorter one by one.

July

A month of hot and humid days,
When storms are likely, the weatherman says,
So choose a spot that's in the shade,
Refresh yourself with lemonade.

A favourite month for flower shows,
The right time of year, I suppose,
Or garden parties on the lawn,
When summery dresses are always worn.

The lovely sound of willow on leather,
(They seem to go so well together),
Is coming from the village green,
Where all the local cricket's seen.

August

Rich August has now all but gone,
The fields are empty, one by one,
The orchard boughs hang thick with crop,
And soon the fruit begins to drop.

The summer sun has had its way,
With leaves and grasses, new-mown hay,
Signs of change are all around,
September impatiently paws the ground.

But she must wait a moment more,
Before she enters through the door,
For August will not yet give way,
Perhaps tomorrow, if not today.

September

Last days of summer pass slowly away,
I saw the fruit pickers earlier today.
The swallows were gathering ready to leave,
For warmer climates, far south, I believe.

The longed-for rain falls steadily down,
And umbrellas add colour in town,
The dust of summer at last is laid,
And colourful flowers begin to fade.

That wonderful light form of sunshine and shade,
Unique to September, has gone I'm afraid.
The paper boy's early, strange to relate,
And dusk creeps upon us well before eight.

October

The hunters' moon, a special sight,
Sits in the sky, an orb of light,
A certain chill is in the air,
And mists are gathering everywhere.

Wind and rain have laid trees bare,
And leaves are scattered everywhere,
A wonderful carpet of gold and brown,
Fit for a queen, an autumn gown.

Animals scurry, aware of their needs,
Nuts and acorns, roots and seeds,
For early frosts will soon be here,
To chill us all this time of year.

November

The days are short, the nights are long,
The wind is playing a wintry song,
Everywhere seems so cold and dreary,
No wonder everyone seems weary.

But wait a moment, we should remember,
A certain date - the fifth of November,
When bonfires blaze to warm the air,
With fireworks exploding everywhere.

And as the month slowly passes away,
We watch the rain, even heavier today.
But tomorrow brings such a nice surprise,
Dry and sunny, a sight for sore eyes.

December

The year is slowly slipping away.
The cold, bleak days are here to stay.
A flurry of snow or driving rain,
Oh when will summer come again?

'What about Christmas?' I hear you say,
'It's only twenty-four days away.'
'Think of the shopping still to be done,
I'm sure that will be a lot of fun!'

The trees are all arrayed with lights,
To help us brighten dreary nights.
The carol singers take their leave,
Reminding us it's Christmas Eve.

Spring

I have this feeling when spring is near,
It always happens this time of year.
No other season can really compare,
With the realisation new life's in the air.

It seems to come with the freshening breeze,
That stirs to life the skeleton trees,
A certain excitement fills the air,
For nature's evolving everywhere.

Green leaves, green shoots and golden flowers,
A view that one could watch for hours,
And soon the new-born lambs appear,
What a wonderful time of year!

Summer

The heavy-scented May is past,
The die of summer now surely cast,
For garlands of flowers pervade the view,
The wonder of summer returns anew.

A boat on the lake or perhaps the river,
The breezes which made the rushes quiver,
The wonderful feeling this season brings,
All cares forgotten for other things.

The azure sky, the rolling sea,
The stretches of sand for you and me,
You ask, 'Why does it have to end?'
The answer as always, 'That's life, my friend.'

Autumn

The mists of autumn linger near,
As night makes way for dawn,
The air is crisp, the sky is clear,
Dew gathers on the lawn.

The yellow orb that is the sun,
Lies waiting in the wings,
It knows it has its course to run,
And then the blackbird sings.

And later on dusk casts its cloak,
And wood smoke fills the air,
Another day for country folk,
Another gem to share.

Winter

Winter at last! I've waited so long,
To feel snowflakes upon my tongue,
To see the trees bedecked in white,
Ghostly on a moonlit night.

The trail that leads me to the wood,
I sense a tingling in my blood,
I enter and to my delight,
A changing filigree of light.

The cold fields beckon, I move along,
The air is clear, the message strong,
That winter, at last, is here to stay,
Until such time as Spring says, 'Away!'

Paul McIntyre

I'm aged 26 and this is my third Spotlight collection. The poems I've written in this collection cover various themes but mostly religious issues.

As I said in my last profile, I think my poems give comfort, reassurance and guidance to people; words are powerful. I pray for a more peaceful world, but in order for it to happen we have to start with ourselves.

I deplore hatred and violence, I don't understand it and don't want to. I think if the world pulled together, religious or not, and treated others how they, themselves, would like to be treated, we'd operate a more positive energy thus helping to stamp out hate and evil.

My last collections - 'New Dawn' and 'An Open Forum' were also on various issues and meant a lot to me but I think I have grown lyrically in this 2004 collection.

God bless, and love to all.

The End Of An Era

If bloodthirsty hands that can curse the lands
To form an ocean that's made up of tears
Then oceans would flood through deserts of blood
So each emotion would drown all my fears

If the sun should fall in a big fireball
The sun could then burn away all the woe
Drying the waters that tears had brought us
The sad tears I yearn to no longer flow

If there were a storm to smother each scorn
Would I surrender to the stormy winds?
Could all these combined cleanse this troubled mind
Cleansing so tender all my past sins?

If crushed by the sky, we'd no longer cry
No waters would shed, but first I would pray
To nature's maker - God our creator
The one who bled for us of today.

Free Spirit

Her soul is shining
Full of love
Her spirit's climbing
Up above
To the heights
Where no man's been
Seeing sights
We've never seen
Like from a dream
Though oh, so real
She now can touch
All we can't feel
Don't cry too much
You're not apart
Though you can't see her
She's in your heart
Her soul is shining
Like a star
Her spirit's soaring
Oh so far
And how it flies
So very free
In heavenly skies
With God she'll be
She's full of glee
As angels sing
In happiness
With God our King
There's loveliness
With magic bliss
She is the one
You'll always miss.

Purer Souls

Life is to test me, mould and interest me
A journey to learn me what's right and wrong
Whilst sharing my loss I'm bearing my cross
To learn is to burn but still carry on

I'm paying my dues, my soul bears the bruise
Whilst learning, I'm yearning to change my heart
I'm learning to give in order to live
Through trying I'm crying when we're apart

Now don't desert me, leave then to hurt me
Surviving though striding to reach my goals
Just learn how to feel, then make me a deal
We'll sit it and be it with purer souls.

The Red Ruby Beads

My present dream is forbidden
When the dream came near I had lied
So now I keep my dream well hidden
Behind the night my dream will hide

My tears have shed through intense guilt
So I will cast aside my needs
As it would spill much more than milk
Like wine in rich red ruby beads

The wine cabinet bares plenty
But still each bottle has to empty

To live my dream would end in tears
We may see blood as our heart bleeds
Amongst the cries that no one hears
Red blood - in rich red ruby beads

For love to grow we plant the seeds
Ignoring pain of poison deeds

In the garden we once shared
Our roses grow amongst the weeds
Roses you'd planted when you cared
Red roses - like red ruby beads

Time will wither all the petals
In place, the sting of long sharp nettles

I'm in my room which we once had
An empty room where sadness breeds
Staring at the paint work drives me mad
Dark red - like rich red ruby beads

But paint work does not last a lifetime
Just like the sun can't always shine

Now I'm watching you walking up the aisle
A wedding is where all this leads
I notice just beneath her smile
A chain - of rich red ruby beads

Our Queen Of England

With speeches to give, long may the Queen live
God bless her with health, joy and affection
As our days unfold, our Queen carved in gold
Be granted in wealth, love and protection

She's blessed by the Lord and truly adored
And as our Queen reigns each God-given year
She waves to the crowd, makes her country proud
As our love remains so greatly with her

As years come around since our Queen was crowned
She does her duty in blue royalty
So by her we stand across our Queen's land
Who's shown us beauty in true loyalty

For when the Queen parts she'll stay in our hearts
Along with her love for life and its zest
Our beloved Queen, so good and serene
From God up above, she'll always be blessed.

Remembrance Sunday

For their God they had done what's right
For family they had to fight
In Heaven with God comes their ascendance
Let's pray in silence for remembrance.

I hope all war will banish some day
I'll pray for this on Remembrance Sunday.

Sacred Grounds

Oh, these are the sands - the soft sacred sands
That cover the ground on our sacred lands
Gold, shimmering dust - a deep breath of lust
Where two lovers stand on gold, sacred sand

I'm holding your hand on soft, sacred sand
And with every grain - our love shuns the rain

And these are the hills, the sweet, holy hills
Oh, so quiet in sound where sweet passion spills
As heavy winds gust - our love is a must
Where sweet passions fill on this sacred hill

As all sadness stills on these sacred hills
We see the time pass on the silken grass

Oh, this is the mountain, evergreen mountain
The place where we lay, with no words to say
We quietly pray - keep pleasures at bay
Then kiss by the fountain - on evergreen mountain

Oh, this is the garden - the place where I harden
I love you so much - when feeling your touch
I harden to sadness - in this world of madness
And feel such pleasure when I'm in your clutch.

Too Late?

The skies turned red with thunder and lightning
Reflecting images of the mad sea
Where people bled in murder so frightening
As evil lurked around you and me.

The ground shuddered, we could see the cracks
And then came the fire from underneath
In an image of virgins on their backs
We felt fear, shock and disbelief.

Then we all felt pain from each other's tears
When witnessing horror we were to create.
We all cried in shame as we faced our fears
But couldn't turn back as now was too late.

A flash of our lives before we were seen
Confusion and terror took over our hearts
Just like a predicted, forgotten dream,
The red sky lowers as the hot ground parts.

We fell to the ground, some dying with fright
As a fate caught up with you and me
All of a sudden there was no more light
As all that was left was a pure black sea

If only we could have another chance . . .

No More War

We don't want history to repeat
As people we can't take much more
There's children with no food to eat
That is why we plea - no more war

We don't want knives, guns or bombs
There's lives been taken we can't restore
No rights can come from all these wrongs
So pray with me - no more war

With thousands falling to their feet
With all the hate and all the gore
Let us show love to whom we meet
So there will be - no more war

As people stumble to the floor
We pray to see - no more war.

God's Gifts

My food is a gift
My friends are a gift
My family's a gift
Past and present
My home is a gift
My pet is a gift
And life is a gift
For the rich and the peasant
The world is a gift
And nature's a gift
My health is a gift
And I will not abuse it
The sun is a gift
And birth is a gift
Kindness is a gift
And I'm going to use it,
I won't be bitter of what I don't have,
Only pray and be grateful for what I've had given,
So if ever I feel alone or bored
I'll remember my gifts
Precious gifts from the Lord.

Remember I Love You

Oriental birds flew from paradise
Such wild, beautiful, colourful birds
They flocked our gardens, brought beauty to life
Then I remembered all those special words . . .

'When birds fly from Heaven on one sweet day
It's a sign that the angels can hear us pray
They send part of Heaven through sunny skies
It's a message of joy as each bird flies.'

Now I realise there is love shining through
Those birds represent the beauty in you
So when all the birds leave the skies of blue
And return to the Heavens -
Remember I love you.

I Say A Prayer

I go to bed and say a prayer
To our Holy Lord above
I sense His presence everywhere
I feel His warmth, His joy and love.

God Is The Greatest Artist

With His apostles He sat at the table
Power until the end of time
With this fine gathering we were able
To drink His blood through the wine -

And eat His flesh through the bread
Once our sweet Jesus bled
So we could all be fed
In acceptance with His praise
Should I change my ways?

Mary Magdalene - once a prostitute
God strengthen me in holiness (Sweet Jesus)
Adam and Eve stole forbidden fruit (from the tree)
Is anybody sinless (God frees us).

Lord show forgiveness, God bring light
Holy Father in thy sight . . .

(This world, the whole nation, the next world,
Is all God's creation. This creative existence is from
Our Lord's heart, this creative existence is His work of art).

God is the greatest artist

Lost Love

The stars are shining so bright and so bold
Like emerald and sapphire encrusted jewels
In a moonlit air, so frosty and cold
That has made a frosted bed of the pools

Your love reminds me of this wintry night
Beautifully special, but so very cold.
Love began warm and felt so right
Until bitter coldness came and took hold.

The moonlit haze that shone bright gold
Cast a line across the night sky
Telling the loveliest story ever told
Like two lovers watching the night go by.

And every night after the days unfold
This place is where I come and spend my time
Now I don't have anyone to hold
All because you are no longer mine.

Times You Won't Forget

Worry not my child
You have your life to live
Wonderland won't last
You'll grow up fast
You have so much to give
Your present times are mild
There's no sign of hatred yet
So have your fun
And don't you run
From times you won't forget.

Spotlight Poets Information

We hope you have enjoyed reading this book - and that you will continue to enjoy it in the coming years.

If you are interested in becoming a Spotlight Poet then drop us a line, or give us a call, and we'll send you a free information pack.

Alternatively if you would like to order further copies of this book or any of our other titles, then please give us a call or visit our website at www.forwardpress.co.uk

Spotlight
Poets

Spotlight Poets Information
Remus House
Coltsfoot Drive
Peterborough
PE2 9JX

Telephone: 01733 898102

Email: spotlightpoets@forwardpress.co.uk